Cast Iron Gourmet

77 AMAZING RECIPES
WITH LESS FUSS AND FEWER DISHES

Megan Keno

FOUNDER OF COUNTRY CLEAVER

PAGE STREET
PUBLISHING CO.

PAGE STREET
PUBLISHING CO.

First published in 2017 by

Page Street Publishing Co.

27 Congress Street, Suite 105

Salem, MA 01970

www.pagestreetpublishing.com

Distributed by Macmillan, sales in Canada by The Canadian Manda Group.

21 20 19 18 17   1 2 3 4 5

ISBN-13: 978-1-62414-412-7

ISBN-10: 1624144128

Library of Congress Control Number: 2017933698

Cover and book design by Page Street Publishing Co.

Photography by Megan Keno

Printed and bound in China

To my little family,
Ben and Huck.

———————○———————

THANK YOU FOR BEING THERE THROUGH THE SUCCESSES, THE MELTDOWNS AND ALL THE DISHES.
MOST OF ALL, THANK YOU FOR MAKING ME LAUGH AND LETTING ME PURSUE MY DREAMS.
YOU, BEN, YOU BOUGHT ME MY FIRST PIECE OF CAST IRON ALL THOSE YEARS AGO . . .
I BLAME YOU FOR THIS AND THANK YOU IN EQUAL MEASURE.

Contents

Preface

Some smarty-pants marriage therapist said that people speak five love languages and that half the battle of a successful marriage is communicating with those you love in a way they can understand. My cooking is my love language. It is how I show my love to those around me. Cooking is definitely a trait that has been passed down to me through my family. Lucky for me. Unlucky for my pant size.

By nature I have always been a baker, but I realized early on that the key to ensuring Ben, my then boyfriend and now husband, would stick around was to make sure there was food he could eat on a daily basis. Unfortunately, it can't all be cookies and cream puffs. I've spent the last six years trying to balance my love of sugar and carbs with trying to cook vegetables and other foods that grow from the ground. Trust me, it wasn't always sunshine and good steaks. At the beginning, I couldn't even make macaroni from a box without it still being crunchy. The horror.

But taking the time to learn, grow and venture out of my cooking bubble gave me a new confidence that I hope you will find in yourself as well.

This book balances two sides of my cooking philosophy—all the tools and expensive pans in the world won't make you a great cook, but mastering the basics will. Simple, comforting dishes are best because you can elevate them with a few quick changes that give them a whole new flavor or purpose. Elevated can be anything you want it to be—elegant, fancy or just dimensional in a way it wasn't before. You'll find down-home classics like Blueberry, Cardamom and Coconut Crumble (page 157), which combines warm spices and summer fruit to transform the summer staple to a rainy-day must-have, and Pork Medallions in Mushroom Cream Sauce (page 54), which is just as comforting as it is elegant. All made in one pan.

Cast iron is known the world over for its high-quality cooking properties, and you can spend as much or as little as your bank account will allow. But focus on finding sturdy, reputable cast iron opposed to budget brands. Inexpensive generic cast iron won't get you the results or have the resiliency that its more reputable counterparts will. Cast iron is an investment, so make it count.

Find the tools that make your job easier so you can hone your craft and be a success.

My goal is to break down the barriers of cast-iron cooking, remove it from grandma status and cement it in our everyday lives again. Beyond bringing it back into fashion, and risk it being a trendy tool that will fade, I hope this book can build your confidence, demystify cast iron and help you become a more versatile cook with fewer dishes to do at the end of the day.

Thank you for entrusting me with your time. This book is my biggest culinary labor of love to date, and I hope you will find it helpful and inspiring in your new cast-iron journey. Most important of all, I hope that you will spread love by sharing good food with those you care about.

Our love languages are the same. I can tell.

Megan Keno

Introduction to Cast Iron

Cast-iron cooking goes way back before your grandma's time. Many of us remember being told stories about grandma's pan or even stories from our grandmas about how they are still cooking with their great-grandma's old cast-iron pan. If you're like me, at the time you heard those stories, the context and gravity were never apparent—why is she attached to using such an old, crusty pan? There are new ones at the store! Nonstick, even! It wasn't until much later that I realized new and fancy was never really the point; it was time.

Cast-iron pans passed down through generations have years of cooking in them. These well-worn and loved pans fry, sear, braise and bake, and just like your grandma, they have stood the test of time, even becoming better with age. This had all been forgotten as new nonstick, lightweight cheap cookware became trendy and all the rage. We've forgotten what we had, but not anymore.

Known for their reliability, durability and heat retention, cast-iron pans are the most versatile tool you can have in your kitchen! Gone might be the days of cooking with cast-iron pots slung over a raging open fire, but the trustworthiness and steadfastness of a cast-iron pan are here to stay.

So why do we use cast iron? Cast iron has remarkable properties that can help any new or seasoned cook advance in their craft. When handled with care, cast-iron pans run laps around their shinier, more expensive cooking pan counterparts. With repeated use and proper care, a thin veil of oil is baked onto the pan, creating a practically nonstick surface, a process called seasoning. No need for nonstick coatings that can wear off or get damaged. Cast iron can do everything better than its more technologically "advanced" buddies. It heats uniformly, retains its heat and gets to temperatures other pans can only dream of. The tastiest steaks are cooked on cast iron. The Cowboy Butter Skillet-Grilled T-Bone Steak (page 63) is proof of that.

TYPES OF CAST IRON

Cast iron is typically found in two varieties: bare cast iron and enameled cast iron. But which one do you need? And when?

Bare cast iron is simple and unpretentious. It takes a little extra love and care that it's enamel-coated buddy does not, but that's not a reason to make you shy away from it. Bare cast iron can be used in all of your cooking applications, from stovetop cooking to oven baking and braising, and you can place it right in the fire for campsite cookouts. It welcomes the use of metal utensils that its coated counterparts run and hide from.

The only downside is that you have to season it. Give it a little extra love. Taking proper care of your bare cast iron will keep it in shape for years to come and stave off the rust that comes with leaving cast iron exposed and unprotected in wet conditions. Even if you find that rust setting in, there are ways to fix it, so don't fear.

Bare cast iron's more colorful cousin, enameled cast iron, can be found in all the same sizes as its bare buddy. Beyond its colorful plumage, there are definite benefits to having a selection of enameled cast iron in your arsenal. The porcelain fired coating on these pans is rock steady and has incredible durability. In certain instances, like when cooking with acidic foods or with aromatic foods that might get locked into bare cast iron, enameled can be the way to go. The porcelain coating doesn't require the seasoning that bare cast iron does, which can be a time saver in the long run. It can go all the places that your bare cast iron can go, save one—the fire. As hard as the porcelain is, there are times it can chip off. So treat enameled cast iron with care, but know it is a powerhouse in your kitchen, too.

SIZE MATTERS

What size pans do you need? This book was specifically written geared toward the Dutch oven and three different sizes of pan: the 10-inch (25-cm), 12-inch (30-cm) and 6-quart (5.5-L). Again and again these pan sizes have proven to be the must-haves for any strong cast iron–based kitchen. Of course, you can always add or subtract pans when you need them and if you're feeding a herd, but these three have been staples in my kitchen, and I know you will find success with them, too.

MONEY HONEY

When it comes to pricing out skillets, it's tempting to go for the bargain-brand cast iron. My argument always comes down to answering this question: What is the best tool for the job? I'm not an advocate for spending money for the sake of spending money. And forking over hundreds of dollars on a new pan that you're not even sure you're going to like is a huge commitment that you could regret. My suggestion is always do your research and find what attributes you hold most dear. Durability, reliability, manufacturing and price all weigh heavily in the decision. But once you find your perfect pan, that's when you go gusto.

French-made cast iron, like Staub and Le Creuset, has been a tried-and-true favorite for generations, and its beautiful color schemes are captivating. American-made Lodge Cast Iron is rustic and focuses on bare cast iron in all shapes and sizes. It even carries a growing line of its own enamelware. Smaller manufacturers pop up periodically, and I encourage you to find what suits you best.

Grazers

Growing up, meat was an imperative in our house, and I love it to this day—even though I spent far too many weekends in my self-conscious teenage years picking fat off my bacon because I thought it would make me fat. Trust me; I have rolled my eyes enough at my former self to go around.

I make no apology for my meat-loving ways, though I am a vegetable convert now. I learned about No-Pit Hawaiian Kalua Pork (page 17) from my brother-in-law's mother, who grew up on Oahu. No pit required, but it has all the flavors of hours under the clay earth! Mama Mel's Ginger Ale Brisket (page 21) is the stuff family holiday memories are made of. I am lucky enough to have been bestowed this recipe to keep Mel's memory alive. I hope that you will find it a wonderful part of your holiday celebrations for years to come. And as a way to stay true to our Czech roots, my mother taught me how to cook the Caraway Seed Slow-Roasted Pork Shoulder (page 14) with cracked caraway seeds, onions and hours of slow roasting in the oven for the tenderest, fall-off-the-bone pork shoulder you will ever have.

I hope these tried-and-true family classics will feed your family and grow some memories.

Apple-Thyme Pork Chops with Hard Cider au Jus

I knew I had to have one pork chop recipe in this book solely because it is my husband's favorite food. Pork chops were one food that until now I had yet to master, or fall in love with. Now I am firmly in Camp Pork Chop. These pork chops are fried in a pan and then roasted with crunchy apples and onions. The whole pan is then deglazed with hard cider, which turns into a delicious au jus for serving. After making this recipe you will also be a pork chop convert!

SERVES: 2 to 4

¼ cup (30 g) flour

½ tsp granulated garlic powder

2 tsp (4 g) lemon thyme, divided

Salt and pepper

2 tbsp (28 g) butter

2 tbsp (30 ml) olive oil

2 (2-in [5-cm])-thick bone-in pork chops

1 apple, peeled and diced

½ cup (76 g) onion, chopped

1 clove garlic, peeled and minced

¾ cup (180 ml) hard cider of choice (I used sweet as opposed to dry, but either would be wonderful.)

Preheat your oven to 350°F (176°C).

In a shallow bowl, whisk together the flour, garlic powder, 1 teaspoon (2 g) of the lemon thyme, salt and pepper. Set this aside. Heat your cast-iron skillet over medium heat, adding in the butter and olive oil. While that heats, take the two pork chops and pat them dry with paper towels to remove any excess moisture. Season the chops with salt and pepper as well. Never be afraid to season!

Dredge the seasoned pork chops in the flour mixture, and tap them gently to remove any excess flour. Place them into the heated skillet and fry until dark golden brown, about 3 to 4 minutes on each side. Monitor them occasionally to ensure they are not burning. Once they are golden brown, remove them from the pan and set them aside on a plate.

Next, add the diced apple and onion to the skillet, and allow them to begin to deglaze the pan and sweat. Stir them occasionally until the apples begin to soften and the onions begin to turn translucent, 7 to 9 minutes. Add the minced garlic and remaining lemon thyme to the pan. Pour in the hard cider to complete the deglazing of the pan. Nestle the pork chops back into the pan alongside the apples and onions, and place them into the oven for 20 to 25 minutes, or until the center of the pork chops reaches 145°F (63°C). Remove from the oven, and allow the pork chops to rest for at least 5 minutes before serving. Don't forget to finish drinking your hard cider!

NOTE: Bone-in pork chops are best for this recipe, but if you can't get them, thick-cut boneless pork chops will do. If you do use thick-cut boneless pork chops, reduce the cooking time slightly. Just make sure they reach the proper internal temperature of 145°F (63°C) before consuming.

Caraway Seed Slow-Roasted Pork Shoulder

If I were ever to find myself in a predicament where I was requesting my last meal, my grandmother's Caraway Seed Slow-Roasted Pork Shoulder would be at the top of the list. Paired with her flawless and fluffy dumplings and sweet-and-sour red cabbage, it's the stuff my dreams are made of. This recipe feeds a crowd, as all good recipes do.

SERVES: 8 to 10

4 lb (1.8 kg) bone-in pork shoulder

Salt and pepper

¼ cup (60 ml) vegetable or canola oil

2 tbsp (14 g) crushed caraway seeds

1 large white or yellow onion, sliced

1½ qt (1.5 L) chicken stock

Take the pork shoulder out of the fridge, and let it sit, covered, on the counter for about 1 hour prior to cooking. This will promote even cooking.

Preheat your oven to 325°F (160°C).

Pat the shoulder dry with several paper towels. Season the pork on all sides liberally with salt and pepper.

On the stove, heat up the vegetable oil in your Dutch oven over medium-high heat until the oil is shimmering in the pan, about 2 minutes. Place the pork shoulder into the pan and allow it to sear on each side until it is golden brown, about 3 to 5 minutes. The pork may stick to the pan but will release on its own. Try not to disturb the meat too much or pull it away from the pan until it naturally releases.

Sprinkle the caraway seeds over the top of the pork shoulder and top with the sliced onion. Some of the seeds and onion may fall off, which is okay; try not to disturb them. Pour the chicken stock into the pan, avoiding washing away the seeds and disturbing the onion on top. Fill the Dutch oven with enough chicken stock to go about halfway up the roast. Cover with the lid of the Dutch oven and place it in the oven to braise for 3 to 4 hours, until the pork is fork-tender and falling off the bone. Serve right from the pan or, if you want a crispier texture, pull it apart with a fork, like you would with pulled pork, place it on a baking sheet and put it back in the oven to crisp for about 5 to 10 minutes.

NOTE: Crush the caraway seeds in a mortar and pestle beforehand to release their aroma. If you don't have one, then place the seeds in a sturdy plastic bag and roll over them with a rolling pin.

No-Pit Hawaiian Kalua Pork

Short of being on vacation in Hawaii, it is hard to come by a Kalua pork shoulder unless you are committed to digging a pit in your own backyard. Handed down to me by my sister's Hawaiian in-laws at her wedding, this is the next best thing. It's as close to the islands as you might get without the long plane ride. It is worth searching out traditional Hawaiian salt for this recipe. Alaea-style salt has red clay in it, true to the islands.

SERVES: 6 to 8

3½–4 lb (1.5–1.8 kg) boneless pork shoulder, known as the butt

2–3 tbsp (36–54 g) Hawaiian or coarse sea salt

1 tsp (2 g) fresh ground pepper

3 tbsp (45 ml) vegetable oil

3 tbsp (45 ml) liquid smoke

½ cup (120 ml) water

1–2 (12-oz [360–720-ml]) cans guava nectar

Remove the pork shoulder from the fridge 1 hour prior to cooking to take the chill off and promote even cooking. Season with salt and pepper on all sides.

Preheat your oven to 300°F (150°C).

Heat your Dutch oven over medium heat, and then add the vegetable oil to the pan and heat until shimmering, about 2 minutes. Sear all sides of the pork to a golden brown, about 3 to 5 minutes, but do not switch sides until the pork naturally releases from the pan.

Sprinkle the pork with the liquid smoke, water and guava nectar. Cover the Dutch oven and place it in the oven. Uncover every hour to baste the pork.

Remove from the oven after 5 to 6 hours, when the pork easily shreds with two forks. Remove the pork from the Dutch oven and let it rest for 20 minutes before completing the shredding. Serve while hot.

Coq au Chardonnay

Coq au vin sounds high and mighty and difficult to make. The beauty of it is that it is a one-pan meal that brings the French countryside to your table. The process of braising breaks down the chicken and infuses it with delicious flavors and comforting smells. Switching from the typical red wine to a chardonnay lightens up the flavors while still leaving this dish just as comforting as the original.

SERVES: 4 to 6

2 tbsp (30 ml) olive oil

4 oz (115 g) bacon, chopped

1 (4-lb [1.8-kg]) fryer chicken, cut into 6–8 pieces

Salt and pepper

2 cups (260 g) baby carrots

8 oz (226 g) sliced button or cremini mushrooms

1 yellow or sweet onion, sliced

2 cloves garlic, minced

2 cups (480 ml) chardonnay

1 cup (240 ml) chicken stock

2½ tsp (5 g) fresh thyme

Preheat your oven to 250°F (120°C).

Heat the olive oil in a large Dutch oven. Add the bacon and cook over medium heat for 6 to 8 minutes, or until crispy. Remove the bacon and drain it on a plate lined with paper towel. Leave the bacon grease in the pan.

Next, pat the chicken pieces dry with a handful of paper towels. Liberally sprinkle the chicken on all sides with salt and pepper. Brown the chicken pieces in batches in the bacon grease for about 5 minutes each, turning the chicken to ensure it browns evenly. Remove the chicken from the Dutch oven, and add it to the same plate as the bacon, until all the chicken is cooked.

Add the carrots, mushrooms, onion, 1 teaspoon (3 g) of salt and ½ teaspoon of pepper into the pan and cook over medium heat for 10 to 12 minutes. Stir until the onions start to turn golden brown, about 5 minutes. Add the garlic and cook until the garlic just becomes fragrant, about 1 minute. Put the bacon, chicken and any juices that collected on the plate back into the pot. Stir in the wine, chicken stock and thyme and bring to a simmer. Cover the pot with a tight-fitting lid and place in the oven for 30 to 40 minutes, until the chicken is tender. Remove from the oven and place on top of the stove. This dish is best when served while hot.

NOTE: For quicker prep, ask your local grocer or butcher to break down your chicken into 6 or 8 pieces. It will save you a lot of fuss!

Mama Mel's Ginger Ale Brisket

When recipes get handed down, they are done so for a reason. This brisket holds a special place in my heart because of the woman whose name it bears. Mama Mel was my best friend Beka's mother. The first Hanukah Beka and I spent together was when I had my first real latkes—and this brisket. Beka has made it every year since, and every year I get to partake in its heritage and love. I'm so lucky to have it here in the book in memory of a very special lady. I hope it will find its way to your table soon.

Cast iron is a brisket's best friend. A good Dutch oven seals in the juices and braising liquid, breaking down the brisket until it's fall-apart tender.

SERVES: 16

---

1 (7-lb [3.2-kg]) flat-cut brisket (not corned)

2 packets dry onion soup mix

6 cloves garlic, minced

3 tsp (8 g) salt

2 tsp (4 g) ground pepper

2 yellow or sweet onions, thinly sliced

2 lb (1 kg) button or cremini mushrooms, sliced

2 tbsp (15 g) whole peppercorns

2 qt (2 L) high-quality ginger ale

Preheat your oven to 325°F (160°C).

With a few paper towels, pat the brisket dry on all sides. Rub all sides of the brisket with the onion soup mix, minced garlic, salt and ground pepper.

In the bottom of the Dutch oven, place half of the onions and mushrooms. Lay the brisket on top, fat side up. Top the brisket with the remaining onions and mushrooms and sprinkle the peppercorns on top. Slowly pour the ginger ale into the Dutch oven, taking care not to splash the brisket too much and wash off the seasoning. Pour ginger ale about halfway up the sides of the brisket.

Cover the Dutch oven, place it into your oven and braise the brisket for 30 minutes. After 30 minutes, reduce the heat to 275°F (135°C) and continue to roast the brisket until it falls apart with a couple of forks. This should take 4 to 6 hours.

Check the brisket every once in a while to make sure there is still ginger ale in the pan, adding a little more if needed. You may or may not use all 2 quarts (2 L).

NOTE: Do not used a precorned brisket for this. Ask your butcher for a noncorned brisket, which is usually available.

Fig-and-Rosemary-Glazed Skillet Chicken

This fig-and-rosemary glaze is a favorite of mine, with its tangy pucker from the balsamic vinegar glaze to its sticky sweetness from the fig preserves. It's a hit in our house every time. One thing that has made this dish easier is that I ask my butcher to break down my chicken into eight pieces, which saves me a lot of time in the kitchen and when the chicken is roasting in the oven. Most butchers will do it for free, just ask!

SERVES: 6

3 cloves garlic, minced, divided

3 sprigs rosemary, destemmed and minced, divided

2 tsp (10 g) salt, divided

1 tsp (2 g) ground pepper, divided

¼ cup (57 g) butter, softened

1 fryer chicken, broken into 6 or 8 pieces

1 cup (240 ml) balsamic vinegar

½ cup (162 g) fig preserves

Preheat your oven to 425°F (220°C).

In a small bowl, mix in half of the garlic, rosemary, salt and pepper with the butter. Place the chicken into the skillet, then gently rub the top of the chicken with the butter mixture. Then place the skillet into the oven to begin roasting.

Pour the balsamic vinegar into a small saucepan and bring it to a low simmer, stirring every few minutes until it has reduced by half and become syrupy, about 20 minutes. Set the balsamic glaze aside to cool until ready to use.

In a small saucepan, combine the remaining herbs with the fig preserves and balsamic glaze. Stir to combine over medium heat until the glaze becomes syrupy, about 5 minutes. Baste the chicken every 5 minutes or so with this glaze. Much of the glaze will likely slide off and into the bottom of the pan, but the glaze will continue to thicken until it becomes sticky. Continue to baste the chicken using the sauce that is now at the bottom of the pan until the chicken thighs reach 165°F (74°C), about 25 minutes. Let the chicken rest for 5 minutes before serving.

Peppered Pork Tenderloin Medallions

The crushed peppercorns, garlic and simple salt let the pork shine through in this fast and easy recipe. You don't have to overcomplicate things to make a memorable meal, and this tender pork tenderloin should be the star of the show.

SERVES: 4

1 (1½-lb [700-g]) pork tenderloin

1 tsp (5 g) salt

1 tsp (5 g) garlic salt

2 tbsp (14 g) crushed peppercorns

¼ cup (60 ml) vegetable oil, divided

Skillet-Roasted Tomatillo Salsa (page 147)

Avocado, for serving, optional

Tomatoes, for serving, optional

Onions, for serving, optional

When you remove the pork from the fridge, pat it dry and remove any silver skin that might be left on the tenderloin.

In a small bowl, mix together the salt, garlic salt and peppercorns. Rub the mixture over the entirety of the pork tenderloin, and allow the pork to rest for 30 minutes so the spices can sink into the meat.

Using a very sharp knife, slice the pork into ¾-inch (2-cm) thick slices, trying to avoid cutting away all the peppercorn crust. If some of it falls off, you can pat it back on.

In your skillet, heat 2 tablespoons (30 ml) of the vegetable oil in a pan over medium-high heat. When the oil starts to simmer, place the medallions in a single layer and reduce the heat to medium. Fry the medallions until they're a deep golden brown on one side, about 3 minutes. Flip all the medallions to the other side and repeat. Remove them from the skillet, and allow them to rest for 5 minutes before serving.

Serve these with Skillet-Roasted Tomatillo Salsa or with freshly sliced avocado, tomatoes and onions.

NOTE: This recipe is a perfect complement to tomatillo salsa. Serve the pork warm with chilled salsa in the summer!

Sweet and Spicy Pineapple-Braised Pork Ribs

These ribs are easy to prepare and will disappear moments after you set them out. You don't have to use pineapple preserves. Experiment and match the flavor of the preserves to the menu you have planned.

SERVES: 8

1 (16-oz [480-ml]) jar of pineapple preserves

2 tbsp (30 ml) Sriracha sauce

2 tbsp (30 ml) soy sauce

2 tbsp (30 ml) sweet chili sauce

2 cloves garlic, minced

3 lb (1.5 kg) country pork ribs

Salt and pepper

Preheat your oven to 300°F (150°C).

In a bowl, whisk together the pineapple preserves, Sriracha sauce, soy sauce, sweet chili sauce and garlic.

Season the pork ribs with salt and pepper on both sides. Place the pork ribs into a Dutch oven or braiser, pour the pineapple mixture in and then nestle the pork ribs into the mixture. Cover and place the Dutch oven or braiser into the oven for 4 hours, opening every hour to turn the pork ribs. Remove from the oven and let the pork ribs rest for 10 minutes before serving.

Gorgonzola and Sun-Dried Tomato Pinwheels

Tangy Gorgonzola and sweet sun-dried tomatoes are a great complement to flank steak. This dish can be prepared ahead of time for a night of entertaining with friends or thrown together quickly on a busy weeknight.

SERVES: 4

2 lb (1 kg) flank steak

Salt and pepper

1 large garlic clove, minced

⅓ cup (80 g) sun-dried tomato preserves or pesto

3–4 cups (90–120 g) fresh spinach

½ cup (120 g) crumbled Gorgonzola or blue cheese

Baker's twine

1 tbsp (14 g) butter

1 tbsp (15 ml) olive oil

Preheat your oven to 400°F (205°C).

Roll out the flank steak and season generously on both sides with salt and pepper. On the top of the flank steak, rub on the minced garlic, then spread the sun-dried tomato preserves over the garlic and sprinkle with fresh spinach leaves and crumbled Gorgonzola or blue cheese.

Tightly roll the flank steak from one end to the other, making sure the ingredients are rolled into the "inside" of the roll. Tie twine around the flank steak horizontally in 2-inch (5-cm) sections. Slice between the twine to create individual pinwheels.

In a skillet, melt together the butter and olive oil. When the butter and oil are bubbling, add the pinwheels, making sure to sear both sides, about 2 minutes a side. Place the skillet into the oven to finish baking the pinwheels until they reach 150°F (65°C) and the cheese is melted, about 10 to 15 minutes. Let them rest for 5 minutes before serving.

Lemon and Herb Chicken with White Wine

The best nights are when you can throw together an elegant meal in one skillet and take all the credit for something that looks like it took hours to prepare. Herbed chicken is seared to get a crispy skin and cooked alongside potatoes to allow all of the flavors to meld into one delicious pan, ready to present as the star of your dinnertime meal.

SERVES: 4

2 tbsp (30 ml) olive oil

1½ lb (680 g) chicken thighs

Salt and pepper

1 tsp (5 g) dried minced onion

2 cloves garlic, minced

1 tsp (2 g) fresh rosemary

1 tsp (2 g) fresh thyme

1 cup (236 ml) low-sodium chicken broth

½ cup (120 ml) white wine of your choice

1 lb (452 g) baby potatoes, cut in half

2 tbsp (30 ml) lemon juice

1 tsp (5 g) cornstarch

Heat your skillet over medium heat, adding in the olive oil and swirling it around in the pan to coat it. Pat the chicken thighs with a wad of paper towels to remove any moisture. This will help the salt and pepper stick to the skin and get the skin crispy. Season both sides of the dried chicken thighs with salt and pepper. Place them skin-side down into the pan to sauté for about 3 minutes per side. When done, the skin should be crispy and golden brown. Remove the chicken and set it aside on a plate. Add the dried onion, garlic, rosemary and thyme to the pan, stirring them together with the remaining olive oil until fragrant. Pour in the chicken broth and wine and whisk to combine everything. Pour the potatoes into the pan, tossing to coat them with the sauce.

Nestle the chicken thighs in between the potatoes and cover the pan. Simmer the potatoes and chicken for about 15 minutes, until the chicken is cooked through and your potatoes are tender. Sprinkle with lemon juice and serve.

If you want to make pan gravy out of the sauce, you can remove the chicken and potatoes, leaving the sauce in the pan. Bring the sauce to a simmer and whisk in the cornstarch until the sauce is smooth. Simmer the sauce until it is thickened, about 3 minutes. Serve it over the chicken and potatoes.

Moroccan Spiced Chicken Wings with Cherry Merlot Glaze

The cinnamon, cumin and pepper in Moroccan seasoning create the base for these sweet and spicy chicken wings. Tart cherry jam and a hearty red wine blend together to create a sticky glaze that makes these wings utterly delightful. If you want to dress up your next game day appetizers or host a dinner party, these wings will make your guests rave for more.

SERVES: 4

1½–2 lb (680–900 g) chicken wings or drums, patted dry

Salt and pepper

1½ tbsp (22 g) Moroccan seasoning blend

1 tbsp (15 ml) vegetable oil

½ cup (160 g) cherry preserves

¼ cup (60 ml) merlot wine

½ tsp ginger

1 large clove garlic, minced

1 tsp (5 ml) Sriracha sauce, optional

1 green onion, cut on the diagonal

Preheat your oven to 475°F (240°C).

Pat the chicken wings dry and liberally sprinkle them with salt, pepper and Moroccan seasoning on all sides. In a skillet over medium-high heat, add the vegetable oil. When the oil starts shimmering, place the wings meat-side down into the skillet. Allow them to brown for 3 to 4 minutes.

While the wings are browning, mix together the cherry preserves, merlot, ginger, garlic and Sriracha. If the mixture is too thick, add more merlot. If the glaze looks thin, don't worry, it will thicken as the wings bake.

After 3 to 4 minutes of simmering, flip the wings in the pan so the meat side is up and brush the wings with the cherry merlot glaze. Place the skillet in the oven for 30 minutes and baste the wings every 10 minutes until they are cooked through and tender. Remove the wings from the oven and set them on a plate. Garnish with green onion. Serve hot.

One-Pot Wonders

No one ends their day excited to do dishes. If you do, please let me know where you get your strength and stamina and if I can buy a bottle of it. I have found myself standing at the sink, staring at a mountain of dishes before me, my eyes glazing over, trying to determine how best to tackle the feat before me. That's when I give up and go watch Netflix and hope Ben catches on. Inevitably it comes down to a battle of wits (i.e., stubbornness), and I end up going back to do them myself. And this further supports the need for a chapter full of one-pot wonders that will allow you to actually relax at the end of your night rather than being elbow deep in dishwater.

Our time with our families is short, and I know I am not alone in this struggle to want to put something comforting and delicious on the table without having to be caught for hours in the kitchen doing dishes afterward. If you are feeding a crowd for breakfast, the Banana, Bourbon and Pecan Baked Oatmeal (page 45) will feed a herd and keep them full. If you want to get out of your comfort zone, the Indian Chicken and Potato Stew with Garam Masala Tomato Sauce (page 38) is out of this world! And the Chorizo Lentil Soup (page 50) is a favorite in our house and a tribute to our Palouse-loving ways. The Palouse is the region in eastern Washington that is known for its rolling hills of superb wheat. My husband grew up there, and we both attended college there. It's how I became "Country Cleaver."

Three Cheese, Sun-Dried Tomato and Spinach Pasta

Sometimes one type of cheese isn't enough! The blend of mozzarella, goat cheese and Parmesan adds to the decadence of this pasta with chicken, sun-dried tomatoes and spinach, making it a well-rounded meal.

SERVES: 6 to 8

12 oz (340 g) collezione or penne pasta

½ tsp onion powder

½ tsp salt

¼ tsp ground pepper

¼ tsp dried thyme

⅛ tsp cayenne pepper

1 lb (453 g) chicken breast, diced

1 tbsp (15 g) butter

1½ cups (100 g) sliced crimini mushrooms

¼ cup (40 g) julienne sun-dried tomatoes

2 cloves garlic, minced

½ cup (120 ml) heavy cream

1 cup (240 ml) whole milk

1 cup (115 g) shredded mozzarella

½ cup (60 g) crumbled goat cheese

½ cup (40 g) shredded Parmesan

2 cups (60 g) fresh spinach

Boil your pasta in an enameled Dutch oven first, and then make your sauce in the same pot. Prepare your pasta according to the package directions, reserving ½ cup (120 ml) of the pasta water for the sauce if needed. Drain the pasta and rinse briefly with cool water to stop the cooking process. Set the pasta aside for later.

While the pasta is boiling, mix together the onion powder, salt, pepper, dried thyme and cayenne pepper in a small dish. Sprinkle the seasoning over the chicken and toss to combine.

In the same Dutch oven you used to boil the pasta, heat the butter. Once it's melted and bubbling, add the chicken, browning it on all sides. This will take about 4 minutes each side. Add the mushrooms and continue to cook until the mushrooms are tender, about 5 minutes. Stir in the sun-dried tomatoes and garlic. Once the garlic is fragrant, about 1 minute, whisk in the heavy cream and milk. Stir in the cheeses until they are melted. Bring the mixture to a simmer, and allow the sauce to thicken slightly, about 5 minutes. If it becomes too thick, slowly add the reserved pasta water until it has reached your desired thickness. Lastly, stir in the fresh spinach until it is wilted. Serve immediately.

Indian Chicken and Potato Stew with Garam Masala Tomato Sauce

If you are new to, or intimidated by, cooking your own Indian-inspired food, this is a wonderful recipe to learn. The flavors are intense, but the cooking techniques are not. This recipe may take time, but the slow braising helps develop the flavors without the need for you to stand guard. If you need a dinner party dish that will please, this is it.

SERVES: 4 to 6

3 tbsp (45 ml) vegetable oil

2 lb (1 kg) boneless, skinless chicken breasts

Kosher salt and freshly ground pepper

1 small sweet onion, chopped

4 garlic cloves, minced

2 tbsp (16 g) finely grated ginger

2 tbsp (30 g) tomato paste

2 tsp (5 g) garam masala

2 tsp (4 g) ground cumin

2 tsp (6 g) ground turmeric

¼ cup (4 g) fresh cilantro, finely chopped, plus more for garnish

3–3½ cups (720–840 ml) low-sodium chicken broth

1 (8-oz [227-g]) can tomato sauce

½ cup (120 ml) heavy cream or plain yogurt

1 lb (452 g) small tri-colored baby potatoes, cut in half if needed

Cilantro, minced

4–6 pieces naan bread

Heat the vegetable oil in your Dutch oven over medium-high heat. While the oil is heating up, season the chicken liberally with salt and pepper. Place it in the oil to fry until it's golden brown on all sides, about 8 to 10 minutes. If the chicken is sticking to the pan, do not fret. The chicken will naturally release on its own when it is browned. You do not want to pull away the browning and leave it behind! Let the chicken tell you when it is done and ready to turn. Once all the chicken is browned, remove it from the pan and set it aside on a plate.

Lower the temperature on the pan to medium low. Without cleaning the pot, add the onion, garlic and ginger, stirring occasionally until the onion is very soft and golden brown, about 5 to 7 minutes. Stir in the tomato paste, masala, cumin, turmeric and cilantro, and stir constantly for 2 to 3 minutes. Whisk in the chicken broth, tomato sauce and the heavy cream or yogurt.

Add the chicken back to the pan and reduce the heat so the stew is simmering. Cover the pan, leaving just a crack for the stew to vent, and simmer for about 1 hour.

Once the hour is up, remove the chicken and use two forks to shred the pieces of chicken. Return the chicken pieces to the pot, and add in the baby potatoes. Continue to simmer the mixture for another 45 minutes to 1 hour, until the potatoes are fork tender.

If the sauce is too thick, add a little additional chicken stock until it reaches your desired consistency. It should be thick, not watery, however. Remove the pan from the stove and serve with a drizzle of added heavy cream or yogurt, minced cilantro and naan bread on the side.

One-Skillet Enchilada Casserole with Cotija and Crema

There is nothing quite like the comforting dishes of your childhood. But sometimes you have to give them a boost to make the memories match your adult taste buds. This enchilada casserole was part of my typical dinner rotation as a kid, and now it is making another appearance in my own home. I added traditional cotija cheese to go with the sharp cheddar and the slightly salty Mexican crema. Your cast iron serves multiple purposes with this recipe, from browning the ground beef to baking the casserole. It's a truly stove-to-table meal.

SERVES: 6

1 lb (454 g) ground beef

1 (28 g) package taco seasoning

1 cup (120 g) chopped yellow onion

1 cup (66 g) chopped cremini mushrooms

2 cups (480 ml) red enchilada sauce

1 (15-oz [425-g]) can pinto beans, drained but not rinsed

2 cups (230 g) cheddar cheese, shredded

½ cup (57 g) shredded cotija cheese

5–6 flour tortillas

Cilantro, minced, for garnish

Mexican crema or sour cream, for garnish

Preheat your oven to 350°F (176°C).

Into your 10-inch (25-cm) skillet over medium heat, add the ground beef and taco seasoning. Cook the ground beef for about 8 to 10 minutes. Next, add the onions and mushrooms to the skillet. Stirring every 2 to 3 minutes, soften the mushrooms and onions. Once the onions and mushrooms are softened, about 5 minutes, stir in the enchilada sauce and pinto beans. Bring the mixture to a simmer, stirring every 2 to 3 minutes. Next, stir in two thirds of the cheddar and cotija cheeses, and mix together until the cheese is melted. Once this is done, pour the beef-and-bean mixture into a mixing bowl and set aside.

Add 1 large spoonful of the beef-and-bean mix, enough to lightly cover the bottom of the skillet, and then press in 1 tortilla. Add 1 more large spoonful of the beef-and-bean mixture, enough to spread a thin layer over the tortilla, and top with another tortilla. Continue layering this way until you nearly reach the top of the skillet, using about 5 or 6 tortillas. Top the last tortilla with any remaining beef-and-bean mixture, and then sprinkle with the remaining cheese.

Bake for 25 to 30 minutes, until the cheese is melted and the edges of the top tortilla look slightly crispy. Remove the skillet from the oven and garnish with minced cilantro and Mexican crema or sour cream.

Pacific Northwest Pan-Seared Salmon with Blackberry Cucumber Salad

Salmon in the summer is the quintessential food of the Pacific Northwest. Whether it's grilled, seared, smoked or put into chowder, we Northwesterners love our salmon. Simple is best when it comes to preparing salmon. You want to let it shine, and it absolutely does when it is paired with a fresh summer-ripened blackberry salad with crunchy cucumber and crumbled feta. It's prepared in an extra mixing bowl, but it's worth it.

SERVES: 4

4 (5- to 6-oz [141- to 170-g]) salmon filets, skin on

¼ cup (36 g) brown sugar

¼ tsp tarragon or thyme

¼ tsp smoked paprika

½ tsp salt

¼ tsp ground pepper

1 English cucumber, seeded and diced finely

1½ cups (216 g) fresh blackberries

½ cup (75 g) crumbled feta

2 tbsp (5 g) minced basil leaves

1 tbsp (15 g) butter

1 tbsp (15 ml) olive oil

Allow the salmon filets to rest on a plate for approximately 20 minutes before you begin cooking. This will help ensure even cooking throughout. While the salmon rests, prepare the brown sugar seasoning by combining the brown sugar, tarragon (or thyme), smoked paprika, salt and pepper in a small dish. Set it aside.

You can also prepare the blackberry salad by combining the diced cucumber, blackberries, crumbled feta and basil. Toss to combine all the ingredients and place them in the fridge to chill until you are ready to serve.

Next, preheat your skillet over medium heat. Prepare your salmon by patting it dry with paper towels and sprinkling the filets with the brown sugar mixture. Melt the butter and olive oil together in the skillet, whisking to combine the two. When the butter is simmering, add each salmon filet skin-side up into the pan, and sear the salmon for about 4 minutes. Reduce the heat under the pan if the sugar begins to burn. Salmon is tender, so avoid poking at it and checking it too often, as it may fall apart more easily and be more difficult to flip. Flip the salmon over onto the skin side and repeat until the salmon reaches at least 145°F (63°C).

NOTE: Substitute other in-season berries like strawberries, huckleberries or blueberries for a regional twist.

Banana, Bourbon and Pecan Baked Oatmeal

The smell of banana and bourbon permeating the kitchen will get you excited to dig into this creamy baked oatmeal. The evaporated milk and half-and-half make it extra creamy, and the bourbon-spiked maple syrup gives it added warmth that is irresistible.

SERVES: 6

2 cups (160 g) rolled oats

1 tsp (4 g) baking powder

½ tsp salt

2 tsp (10 g) ground cinnamon

¼ cup (57 g) unsalted butter, melted and cooled

2 tsp (10 ml) vanilla extract

⅓ cup (78 ml) bourbon-infused maple syrup

¼ cup (59 ml) bourbon

1 egg

1 (12-oz [355-ml]) can evaporated milk

¼ cup (60 ml) half-and-half

2 medium bananas, overripe

½ cup (75 g) chopped pecans

Cream, for serving, optional

Preheat your oven to 350°F (176°C).

In your seasoned skillet, add the rolled oats, baking powder, salt and ground cinnamon. Whisk the oats together. Add the melted butter, vanilla extract, maple syrup, bourbon (if using), egg, evaporated milk, half-and-half, bananas and chopped pecans. Whisk everything together until combined. Make sure the bananas are overly ripe to get the most sweetness out of them. If your bananas are not overripe, put them in the freezer the night before, and then let them thaw before using the next day. This will speed up the ripening process.

Place the skillet into the oven and bake for 35 to 45 minutes or until the top is gently crusted and the mixture is not runny. Let the mixture set for 5 to 10 minutes before serving. Serve in a bowl, with cream drizzled over the top if desired.

NOTE: If you don't have evaporated milk on hand, use milk and add an extra tablespoon (14 g) of butter. And if you can't find bourbon maple syrup, add a shot (1.5 ounces [44 ml]) of bourbon to the mix with regular maple syrup.

Venison-and-Mushroom-Stuffed Manicotti

My family is a hunting family whose year revolves around opening day of deer season. It's been an annual tradition for my family to hunt in the same spots on the mountain for over 70 years. And when one person is successful, we all share the bounty. This year I got a package of ground venison that was a wonderful match for this rich manicotti. If venison isn't to your taste, or in your freezer, ground beef is a perfectly acceptable substitute.

SERVES: 6 to 8

12 oz (339 g) manicotti shells

1 tbsp (15 ml) olive oil

8 oz (226 g) ground venison or beef

1 tsp (5 g) Italian seasoning

½ tsp salt

¼ tsp ground pepper

2 cloves garlic, minced

4 oz (113 g) crimini mushrooms, finely chopped

1 (15-oz [425-g]) container whole fat ricotta

1 egg

½ cup (40 g) shredded Parmesan cheese

1 (6-oz [170-g]) package frozen spinach, thawed and squeezed of excess moisture, chopped

1½ cups (168 g) shredded mozzarella, divided

1 (24-oz [680-g]) jar prepared marinara sauce, divided

Preheat your oven to 375°F (190°C).

In a braiser filled with salted water, cook the pasta according to package directions. Drain and rinse to stop the cooking process. Set the shells aside. Add the olive oil to the braiser. When the oil is heated, add the venison and sprinkle with Italian seasoning, salt, pepper and garlic. Brown for about 5 minutes. Add the diced mushrooms and stir until softened, about 3 minutes. Pour the meat into a large mixing bowl.

In the mixing bowl with the venison and mushrooms, stir in the ricotta, egg, Parmesan, chopped spinach and 1 cup (115 g) of the mozzarella. Gently stuff each manicotti with the mixture.

In the bottom of the braiser, add 1 cup (226 g) of marinara sauce and spread evenly over the bottom of the pan. Place each stuffed manicotti into the pan in a single layer. Cover the pasta with the remaining marinara sauce, and sprinkle the top with the remaining shredded mozzarella cheese. Bake the dish uncovered for about 30 minutes or until the mozzarella is melted and browned on top. Serve hot.

Boursin and Bacon Potatoes au Gratin

There is nothing quite like digging into a dish of cheese-drenched potatoes during the holiday season. This dish is slathered in rich herbed Boursin cheese that gets into every layer. The fact of the matter is that bacon makes everything better, especially cheesy potatoes. This skillet goes from oven to table in rustic style, staying hot with cast iron's amazing heat retention. Keep those taters hot!

SERVES: 8

3 large Yukon gold potatoes

3 large red potatoes

2 tbsp (28 g) butter

1 sweet onion, thinly sliced

3 cloves garlic, minced

½ lb (226 g) bacon

1½ cups (180 g) shredded white cheddar cheese

4 oz (113 g) Boursin cheese

1 cup (240 ml) cream

½ cup (120 ml) whole milk or half-and-half

Preheat your oven to 375°F (190°C).

Using a mandoline or a food processor with the slicing attachment, slice all of your potatoes into even slices. I prefer mine to be about 1⁄16 inch (2 mm) thick.

In the skillet, melt the butter. Once the butter is melted and sizzling, add the onion and caramelize until golden brown, about 10 to 12 minutes. During the last 1 minute of caramelizing the onion, add the garlic and sauté until fragrant. Remove from the skillet and fry the bacon if you have not done so previously. Remove the bacon and drain on a paper towel–lined plate. Wipe out the remaining bacon grease, but do not wash the pan.

In the skillet, layer half of the sliced potatoes onto the bottom. Cover the first layer with half of the caramelized onion and bacon, sprinkling the cheeses over the top. Repeat the second layer the same as the first, topping it with the remainder of the onions and bacon. Pour the cream and milk over the top. Sprinkle with extra cheese, if desired.

Cover the skillet with aluminum foil and place in the oven for approximately 90 minutes, checking after 60 minutes to see if the potatoes are tender through. Remove the skillet from the oven and allow it to cool for 10 minutes before serving.

NOTE: Use other soft cheese varieties like goat cheese for a different flavor!

Chorizo Lentil Soup

On dreary days, this soup paired with a grilled cheese sandwich and a *Harry Potter* marathon is where it's at! My husband and I work opposite shifts, so we don't have a lot of time to whip up a full dinner every night. This recipe makes enough for a hearty family meal, or you can make it for two and have a few days of leftovers.

SERVES: 8

1 tbsp (14 g) butter

1 tbsp (15 ml) olive oil

1 medium red onion, chopped

3 cloves garlic, minced

2 cups (140 g) cubed butternut squash

½ lb (227 g) chorizo pork sausage

1 (28-ounce [794-g]) can fire-roasted crushed tomatoes

2 tbsp (30 ml) chipotle paste or adobo sauce, add more or less to taste

1 (15-oz [425-g]) can black beans, drained but not rinsed

3½ cups (840 ml) chicken stock

1 cup (200 g) dried green lentils

2 tsp (4 g) cumin

2 tsp (4 g) chili powder

Sour cream, for topping

Cilantro, minced, for garnish

In a Dutch oven over medium-high heat, melt the butter and olive oil together until simmering. Add the red onion and sauté until golden brown, about 5 minutes. Next, stir in the minced garlic until it becomes fragrant, about 30 seconds. Add the butternut squash and sauté, stirring every 2 minutes until the edges are golden brown and the squash just begins to soften, about 6 to 7 minutes. Next, move the squash to the side of the Dutch oven and add the chorizo. Using a wooden spoon, break the chorizo into small pieces. Once the chorizo is browned, about 10 minutes, stir in the crushed tomatoes, chipotle paste, black beans and chicken stock. Lastly, add the lentils, cumin and chili powder.

Bring the mixture to a simmer and cover. Let cook until the butternut squash and lentils are both soft, about 40 to 45 minutes. Serve warm with sour cream and cilantro if desired. Corn bread never hurts, too.

Thai Red Curry Chicken Meatballs

Light and packed with flavor, these meatballs are splendid on their own or tossed with zucchini noodles for an Asian fusion like Thai spaghetti and meatballs. The cast iron browns these meatballs on the outside beautifully, sealing in the Thai flavors for the perfect bite-size appetizer or meal.

SERVES: 4 to 6

MEATBALLS

1 lb (453 g) ground chicken

½ cup (35 g) panko bread crumbs

2 cloves garlic, minced

1½ tsp (5 g) ginger, minced

1 egg

½ tsp salt

¼ tsp pepper

¼ tsp crushed red pepper flakes

2 tbsp (2 g) cilantro, chopped

THAI RED CURRY SAUCE

1 tbsp (15 ml) olive oil

2 cloves garlic, minced

1 tsp (5 g) ground ginger, minced

2 tbsp (31 g) red curry paste

1 cup (237 ml) coconut milk

1 tsp (5 g) Sriracha

¼ tsp pepper

¼ tsp salt

¼ tsp red pepper flakes

1 tbsp (1 g) cilantro, chopped

1 tsp (5 ml) lime zest

1 tbsp (15 ml) lime juice

4 small zucchini, spiraled into noodles (optional)

THE MEATBALLS

Preheat your oven to 400°F (205°C).

Lightly spray the skillet or braiser with nonstick spray.

In a large bowl, add all of the meatball ingredients, mixing just to combine. Do not overmix them so they become tough. Using a cookie scoop, create 18 to 24 meatballs. Place the meatballs in a skillet and cook for 15 to 20 minutes or until caramelized on the outside and cooked through, flipping them halfway through to brown on both sides. When done, take the meatballs out of the oven and set them aside on a large plate.

THE THAI RED CURRY SAUCE

Heat the olive oil over medium heat in the skillet you used to bake the meatballs. Add garlic and ginger and cook for 1 minute until the garlic becomes fragrant. Whisk in the red curry paste and cook for an additional minute. Slowly whisk in the coconut milk and continue whisking until the mixture thickens, about 4 minutes. Stir in the Sriracha, pepper, salt, red pepper flakes, cilantro, lime zest and lime juice. If you're adding zucchini noodles, toss them into the sauce and bring the mixture to a simmer for 1 minute to cook the zucchini through. Add the meatballs and toss them to coat them with the sauce. Garnish with extra cilantro if desired. Serve immediately.

Pork Medallions in Mushroom Cream Sauce

This is a perfect dinner for a date night in. Surprisingly luxurious, this one-dish meal doesn't take all night to prepare. And who has time for dishes on date night? Not you! The pork tenderloin medallions stay tender after a quick simmer in this rich mushroom cream sauce. You can serve this over rice, mashed potatoes or egg noodles for a complete meal.

SERVES: 4

¼ cup + 2 tbsp (47 g) flour, divided

Salt and pepper

2 tbsp (30 g) Italian seasoning

1–1½ lb (453–680 g) pork tenderloin

4 tbsp (60 g) butter, divided

2 tbsp (30 ml) olive oil

½ large onion, thinly sliced

8 oz (226 g) button or cremini mushrooms, sliced

3 cloves garlic, minced

1 cup (236 ml) chicken broth

½ cup (120 ml) half-and-half

Preheat your oven to 350°F (176°C) and at the same time, begin heating your skillet over medium heat on the stovetop.

In a bowl, whisk together ¼ cup (31 g) of the flour, salt, pepper and Italian seasoning. Set the plate aside and turn to the tenderloin. Slice the tenderloin into ½-inch (1.5-cm)-thick slices. Season the tenderloin slices with salt and pepper.

In your heated skillet, add in 1 tablespoon (15 g) of butter and 1 tablespoon (15 ml) of olive oil. Melt them together and allow them to come to a simmer. Add the onion and mushrooms, sautéing until golden brown, about 5 minutes. During the last minute of sautéing the onions and mushrooms, add the garlic, cooking it until it is fragrant. Remove the mushrooms, onions and garlic from the pan and set aside on a plate.

Place the skillet back on the stove. Add 1 tablespoon (15 g) of butter and 1 tablespoon (15 ml) of olive oil to the pan and melt until simmering. Dredge each pork medallion in the flour mixture. Fry each medallion until golden brown, about 2 minutes per side. Remove the medallions from the pan and repeat with the remaining medallions.

Sprinkle the remaining 2 tablespoons (16 g) of flour and 2 tablespoons (30 g) of butter into the pan to soak up the juice from the pork. Whisk in the chicken broth and half-and-half until smooth. Bring the mixture to a simmer, whisking constantly. Add the onions, mushrooms and pork medallions back into the sauce. Place the skillet into the oven and bake for 15 to 20 minutes or until the sauce is thickened and the pork medallions reach 160°F (71°C). Serve immediately.

Chocolate-Orange Baked French Toast

Whatever you choose to call this, baked French toast or bread pudding, it all means the same thing to me—custardy soaked bread with cinnamon, chocolate and a hint of orange, aka heaven. I grew up never understanding the allure of it until I started making it on my own. The possibilities are endless, just as are the number of reasons to make it. Bring this out for your family weekend brunch, cart it to a potluck for dessert or eat it warm straight out of the pan. Just make sure you make this. I use an extra mixing bowl for this recipe because it makes coating the bread easier.

SERVES: 8

1 cup (240 ml) half-and-half

1 pt (489 ml) whole milk

1 cup (200 g) brown sugar

8 egg yolks

1 tsp (5 ml) vanilla extract

1 tbsp (17 ml) rum extract

½ tsp salt

1 large orange, zested

1 tbsp (7 g) cinnamon

1 loaf egg bread, cut into 1-inch (2.5-cm) cubes or ½-inch (1.5-cm) slices

1 cup (175 g) chocolate chips

Preheat your oven to 350°F (176°C).

In a large bowl, whisk together the half-and-half, milk, brown sugar, egg yolks, vanilla, rum extract, salt, orange zest and cinnamon.

Place the cubed or sliced bread into a lightly sprayed skillet. If you are using cubes, pour half of them in, top with half of the chocolate chips, and then continue with the remaining bread cubes, topping those with the second half of the chocolate chips. If you are using slices, strategically place them on the bottom of the pan, layering the bread so that the next layer covers the seams, or gaps, of the layer below. Sprinkle chocolate chips between the layers as you go.

Pour the milk mixture over the bread, and let the bread-and-milk mix rest for about 10 to 15 minutes. Gently press down on the bread if the top layers are not getting saturated with the milk mixture. Place the whole skillet into the oven, and bake for 35 to 40 minutes until the internal temperature reaches 165°F (75°C).

NOTE: It's best to use day-old bakery bread for this. The custard soaks in better and the bread doesn't disintegrate.

Macaroni and Cheese Five Ways

I grew up as a blue-box macaroni connoisseur. Thank goodness my palate grew up along with me. Even if I do dabble in the boxed stuff from time to time, my true love lies in the golden roux and cheesy sauce of a real tried-and-true macaroni and cheese. This is my go-to base that builds all my other macaroni and cheese dishes. Building on this base are five different variations that will make all the palates at the table jump for joy.

SERVES: 4 to 6

MACARONI AND CHEESE

4 tbsp (56 g) butter

4 tbsp (30 g) flour

½ tsp ground mustard

2 cups (240 ml) whole milk

1½ tsp (3 g) ground pepper

2½ cups (330 g) cheddar cheese

12 oz (340 g) penne or other pasta of choice, prepared using package directions

VARIATIONS

GREEN CHILI AND PEPPER JACK

1 (4-oz [113-g]) can diced green chiles, drained

Swap cheddar cheese for pepper jack cheese.

ROASTED GARLIC AND SMOKED GOUDA

5–6 large garlic cloves, roasted

Swap half of the cheddar cheese for smoked gouda.

BUTTERNUT SQUASH AND WHITE CHEDDAR

½–¾ cup (225–340 g) butternut squash puree

Swap cheddar cheese with sharp white cheddar cheese.

PROSCIUTTO AND SAGE WITH WHITE CHEDDAR

4 oz (113 g) chopped prosciutto, fried

1–2 tbsp (2–4 g) sage, minced and fried (adjust to taste)

Swap cheddar cheese for sharp white cheddar cheese.

In your cast-iron skillet or Dutch oven, melt the butter until it simmers. Whisk in the flour to form a paste (roux), and allow it to toast until golden brown, whisking constantly, about 4 minutes. Whisk in the mustard powder.

Slowly whisk in the milk to create a smooth béchamel sauce. Whisk in the ground pepper and cheese. Stir the cheese until it's melted and a sauce forms. Whisk in your chosen ingredients. Fold in the prepared pasta and serve.

Thirty Minutes or Less

We are all looking for the best ways to make meaningful meals in a short amount of time. What you don't want to do is while away your hours in front of the stove when the memories you could be making with your family are happening in the other room. These recipes focus on whole, seasonal ingredients that will disappear as soon as your family sits down to eat.

For the meat lovers in your life, Goat-Cheese-Stuffed Chicken Thighs (page 67) is perfect for the weeknight. The Roasted Fall Squash and Sausage Skillet (page 64) pleases the seasonal food fans with a blend of delicata squash, roasted tomatoes, sweet onion and slices of chicken apple sausage. And if you want a little secret, it makes an excellent breakfast with a fried egg on top. Don't forget the spicy sauce!

There may never be enough time in the day, but we all have to make the most of the time we have together. If sitting around the dinner table is all the time your family has together, I hope it is made memorable with these recipes.

Cowboy Butter Skillet-Grilled T-Bone Steak

The best steaks come out of cast-iron skillets. With their ability to get superhot, they can sear the outside of a steak, sealing in all the juicy deliciousness that you crave and rendering the flavors and fats that make a steak truly something otherworldly. Topping off your steak with crumbled Gorgonzola and herbed butter never hurts either.

SERVES: 2 to 4

1 (2-lb [900-g]) T-bone steak, or 2 (1-lb [453-g]) bone-in rib eye steaks

7 tbsp (105 g) butter, softened, divided

1 clove garlic, minced

½ tsp lemon zest

2 tsp (3 g) minced parsley

⅛ tsp ground pepper

¼ tsp red pepper flakes

Kosher salt and pepper

3 tbsp (45 ml) light olive oil

2–3 sprigs thyme

2–3 sprigs rosemary

3 whole unpeeled cloves garlic

½ cup (60 g) crumbled Gorgonzola

Bring the steaks out at least 45 minutes prior to cooking to take the chill off. This will promote even cooking. Preheat your oven to 350°F (176°C).

In a small bowl, mix together 4 tablespoons (60 g) the butter, garlic, lemon zest, parsley, ground pepper and red pepper flakes. When mixed completely, wrap it gently in parchment paper and create a roll out of it. Twist the ends of the parchment paper closed and place it back in the fridge for later. You can also make this ahead of time and keep it in your fridge for just this occasion!

Bring your skillet to temperature slowly starting at medium heat and then turning up to medium-high heat. This will ensure that your pan heats evenly without creating hot spots. Pat the steaks dry with paper towels and season with salt and pepper. Melt 3 tablespoons (45 g) of butter and 3 tablespoons (45 ml) of olive oil together until they are combined and simmering. If you notice the pan starting to smoke too heavily, reduce the heat slightly. If the butter or oil scorches, start over. Sear the steak in the pan for about 4 to 5 minutes per side until it naturally releases from the pan and is a deep golden brown. Do not disturb the steak or check it for doneness too frequently. If the steak does not release from the pan naturally, let it continue to sear until it does. Flip the steak and place it on a portion of the skillet that it previously did not cover, if it is available. You want to give it a fresh hot place to sear. Repeat this. Place the sprigs of thyme and rosemary into the pan, along with the whole garlic cloves.

Next, place the skillet into the oven and bake the steak until it is done to your liking. The thickness of the steak will determine how long it needs to be in the oven. For a 2-inch (6-cm) T-bone steak: 20 minutes for medium rare and 25 minutes for medium. If you are cooking rib eyes, reduce the bake time by 5 to 7 minutes. Remove the steak from the oven and allow it to rest for at least 5 minutes before slicing and serving. Spoon any juices from the pan back onto the steak as it rests. Slice the herbed cowboy butter and place a couple of pats on top of the steak to melt. Top with crumbled Gorgonzola cheese and serve.

Roasted Fall Squash and Sausage Skillet

There is not much I love more in fall than squash. There are so many varieties that lend themselves to phenomenal dishes, and their versatility is unmatched. Delicata squash is one of my favorites because of its low-maintenance cooking. You don't have to peel it because the skin softens as it cooks, so you can eat it all. Add in some sausage, tomatoes, onion and garlic (duh!), and this one-skillet dish is as healthy as it is comforting.

SERVES: 6

1 large delicata squash, seeded and cubed (no need to peel)

1 (12-oz [340-g]) package chicken-and-apple sausage, or other variety of choice, sliced diagonally

1 whole sweet onion, halved and sliced

1 cup (150 g) whole cherry tomatoes

2 cloves garlic, minced

2–3 tbsp (30–45 ml) olive oil

Salt and pepper

1 tsp (1 g) fresh rosemary, chopped

Preheat your oven to 425°F (220°C).

In a large skillet or enameled casserole dish, add the squash, chicken-and-apple sausage, onion, tomatoes and garlic and toss with olive oil. Sprinkle with salt, pepper and chopped rosemary. Roast the vegetables until the squash has softened and the sausage slices are cooked through, about 15 to 20 minutes. Serve hot, straight out of the pan.

If you are in the mood, try butternut or acorn squash as an alternative to delicata. They require peeling before roasting, so it may take a few extra minutes in the prep stages.

NOTE: I'm a firm believer that everything is better with an egg on top. Use your leftovers for breakfast with a sunny-side-up egg!

Goat-Cheese-Stuffed Chicken Thighs

Crispy chicken thighs stuffed with creamy goat cheese and herbs are the way to anyone's heart. Goat cheese, with sun-dried tomatoes, artichokes and spinach is a superb way to dress up a regular weeknight meal or make it special for a date night in. Bone-in, skin-on chicken thighs work best for this recipe.

SERVES: 4

1½ lb (680 g) chicken thighs

¼ cup (55 g) wilted spinach, squeezed of excess moisture

¼ cup (50 g) drained marinated artichokes, finely chopped

2 tbsp (20 g) marinated sun-dried tomatoes, finely chopped

⅓ cup (40 g) goat cheese crumbles

¼ cup (56 g) softened cream cheese

¼ tsp salt

¼ tsp ground pepper

3 tbsp (45 ml) olive oil

½ cup (120 ml) chicken broth

Remove the chicken from the fridge at least 20 minutes before cooking to allow it to come up to room temperature and take the chill off for even cooking. The bone acts as an insulator, so a cold bone will prevent the meat nearest the bone from cooking at the same rate as the surrounding meat.

Preheat your oven to 350°F (176°C).

In a bowl, stir together the spinach, marinated artichokes, sun-dried tomatoes, goat cheese, cream cheese, salt and pepper.

Pat the chicken dry with a handful of paper towels and season the chicken with salt and pepper.

Gently spoon the goat cheese filling under the skin of the chicken and pull the skin taught over the chicken. If it won't stay, use a toothpick to secure the skin.

Preheat the olive oil in a pan over medium heat on the stove. Place the chicken skin-side down in the pan. Cook the chicken until it is dark golden brown and crispy, about 4 minutes. You don't want tear the skin and lose the filling. Using tongs, turn the chicken over and cook on the other side until it's dark golden brown, about 4 minutes. If the chicken is sticking to the pan, let it continue to fry until it releases naturally.

Pour the chicken broth into the bottom of the pan, carefully cover the pan with aluminum foil and place it in the oven for 12 to 15 minutes, or until the internal temperature of the chicken reaches 160°F (71°C). Remove the pan and let the chicken rest for 5 minutes before serving.

Roasted-Vegetable-Stuffed Portobello Mushrooms

With fresh spinach, sweet roasted red pepper, a sprinkling of shallots, marinara and cheese on top, these stuffed portobello mushrooms are the perfect meatless main dish in 30 minutes or less. We are all trying to find ways to eat healthier without sacrificing flavor, and this one does it on all fronts. Use a mixture of your favorite cheeses to suit your needs, or substitute other vegetables when you are having a "clean out the fridge" kind of night. Easy and elegant all in one.

SERVES: 4

8 oz (227 g) fresh spinach

½ cup (170 g) chopped roasted red peppers

¼ cup (40 g) shallot or red onion, minced

⅛ tsp crushed red pepper

½ tsp onion powder

Salt and pepper

4 portobello mushrooms, of even size, stem and gills removed

1 cup (250 g) jarred marinara sauce

1½ cups (168 g) shredded cheese of your choice, such as mozzarella, cheddar or Parmesan

Preheat your oven to 425°F (220°C).

In your skillet over medium heat, wilt the spinach and place it into a mixing bowl to cool.

When the spinach is cool enough to handle, squeeze out any excess moisture and roughly chop. Place the spinach back into the mixing bowl along with the roasted red peppers and shallot. Add the crushed red pepper, onion powder, salt and pepper. Mix together and fill each of the portobello mushrooms with the mixture. Top with marinara sauce and sprinkle each mushroom with cheese. Place them in the skillet and bake for 20 minutes or until the cheese is melted and bubbling and the mushrooms are fork-tender. Serve immediately.

Honey Dijon Turkey Tenderloin

If you are looking for a lean protein to fill you up without weighing you down, turkey tenderloins are here to save the day. They are light enough to let the flavors and seasonings shine through without stealing the show, and they cook in a hurry, which is great for any weeknight warrior.

SERVES: 4

1½ lb (680 g) turkey tenderloin, patted dry

Salt and pepper

¼ cup (60 ml) high-quality Dijon mustard

2 tbsp (30 ml) honey

2 tsp (2 g) minced rosemary

4 tbsp (60 ml) olive or vegetable oil, divided

1½ lb (680 g) tri-color baby potatoes, cut in half

1 tbsp (2 g) dried herb mix, such as parsley, thyme, shallot, garlic

Pat your turkey tenderloin dry with a handful of paper towels and season all sides liberally with salt and pepper. Then place the turkey into a zip-top plastic bag. In a small bowl, whisk together the Dijon mustard, honey, minced rosemary and 3 tablespoons (45 ml) of the oil. Pour the mix over the turkey and zip the plastic bag closed, removing as much air as possible from the bag. Gently massage the bag to make sure all the turkey is covered in the marinade and place in the fridge for 1 hour. If you are busy, this marinade can stay on the turkey overnight or even for two days.

Allow the turkey to sit on a plate at room temperature for 30 minutes prior to cooking. This will ensure the meat cooks evenly.

Preheat your oven to 400°F (205°C).

Place the potatoes in a skillet and toss with the remaining 1 tablespoon (15 ml) of oil and the dried herbs. Nestle the turkey into the potatoes, and place the skillet into the oven for 25 minutes. Check the temperature with an instant-read thermometer. Let the turkey rest for 5 minutes prior to slicing and serving.

NOTE: This recipe works equally well with pork tenderloin or chicken breasts.

Crispy Chicken Thighs

Chicken is so versatile, but a piece of chicken from a pan hardly has any wow factor. This one does. Using bone-in chicken thighs keeps it super juicy.

SERVES: 4

4 bone-in, skin-on chicken thighs, approximately 1½ lb (680 g)

2 tsp (12 g) kosher salt

1 tsp (5 g) ground pepper

½ tsp powdered garlic

¼ tsp paprika

3 tbsp (45 ml) olive oil

½–¾ cup (118–177 ml) low-sodium chicken broth

Preheat your oven to 350°F (176°C).

Remove the chicken from the fridge at least 20 minutes before cooking to allow it to come up to temperature and take the chill off for even cooking. The bone acts as an insulator, so a cold bone will prevent the meat nearest the bone from cooking at the same rate as the surrounding meat.

In a small bowl, whisk together the seasonings and set aside. In your cast-iron skillet, preheat the olive oil on the stove over medium-high heat. While the oil is heating, season all sides of the chicken thighs with the seasoning you just made. Place the chicken skin-side down in the oil in the pan. Cook the chicken for about 4 minutes, or until the chicken is dark golden brown and crispy. If the skin hasn't released from the pan by itself and is sticking, let it continue to cook. It will release on its own; sometimes you just need to be patient. Using tongs, turn the chicken over and cook on the other side until dark golden brown, about 4 minutes. Pour the chicken stock into the bottom of the pan, carefully cover the pan with aluminum foil and place in the oven for about 15 minutes, or until the internal temperature of the chicken reaches 160°F (71°C). Remove the skillet, and let the chicken rest for 5 minutes before serving.

Chorizo and Shrimp Paella

One of my family's traditions is serving nontraditional foods on the holidays. One year we had an authentic paella with all the fixings, from chorizo to mussels to chicken and squid. Now, I'm not the biggest seafood lover in our family—I leave that to my stepdad. But this paella, with shrimp and chorizo, is a perfect balance for seafood and meat lovers alike. It's been simplified to be weeknight friendly and has the flavors you crave without spending all day at the stove. Though this has tomatoes in it, you can use a straight cast-iron skillet if you don't have an enameled one handy. This dish cooks quickly enough that the acid of the tomatoes shouldn't affect the flavor.

SERVES: 6

½ lb (226 g) sliced chorizo sausage

¼ cup (60 ml) olive oil

1½ cups (295 g) arborio rice

3 cloves garlic, minced

Pinch of cayenne pepper

½ cup (120 ml) white wine

1½–2 cups (180–240 ml) chicken stock

1 (15-oz [411-g]) can diced tomatoes

½ lb (226 g) peeled and deveined medium shrimp

1 cup (150 g) peas

1 tsp (5 g) chipotle paste (optional)

Over medium-high heat, add your chorizo to the skillet and cook until crispy and brown on all sides, about 5 minutes. Once the chorizo is cooked, put it aside on a plate. Add the olive oil to the pan, and reduce the heat to medium low. Sprinkle in the arborio rice, and stir to toast the rice, about 5 minutes. Stir in the garlic and cayenne until just fragrant. The rice should look slightly translucent and toasted golden brown.

Deglaze the pan by pouring the white wine into the pan and stirring the rice with the wine. Allow the wine to evaporate, and then whisk in the chicken stock and tomatoes. Cover the pan and cook the rice for about 11 to 12 minutes, until the rice is almost cooked through.

Stir in the shrimp, chorizo and peas, and continue to cook covered for another 6 minutes or until the shrimp is cooked through and the peas are tender. If you want a little extra kick, stir in an additional teaspoon (5 g) of chipotle paste. Serve hot.

NOTE: Add in chicken wings, mussels or clams for added flavor and to up the authenticity while still keeping it great for the midweek.

Bacon-Wrapped Filet Mignon

If everything is better with bacon, then filet mignon with bacon is a transcendent experience. The best way to cook a steak, in my humble opinion, is in a cast-iron skillet. This takes everyone's favorite cut of meat and makes it better with thick-sliced applewood smoked bacon.

SERVES: 4

4 (6–7 oz [170–200 g]) filet mignons

Salt and pepper

4–8 slices applewood smoked bacon, or any thick-cut bacon you can find

2 tbsp (30 g) butter

1 tbsp (15 ml) olive oil

1 cup (66 g) sliced cremini mushrooms

2 sprigs fresh rosemary

2 sprigs fresh thyme

2 cloves garlic, unpeeled

Preheat your oven to 425°F (220°C).

While the oven preheats, pat the steaks dry with a handful of paper towels. Season the steaks on both sides with salt and pepper. Wrap each steak with 1 or 2 pieces of bacon, making sure each steak is well wrapped. Secure the bacon with toothpicks, but do not pierce the beef if you can help it. Not piercing the filets will keep the juices inside the meat.

Heat the butter and olive oil together in a cast-iron pan until they are shimmering. Ensure that the whole bottom of the pan is covered, swirling the pan if you need to. Add the filets to the pan and sear them on each side until they naturally release from the pan, about 2 to 3 minutes per side. Once you flip the filets, place the mushrooms, rosemary, thyme and unpeeled garlic around the steaks. Using a spoon, toss the juices and butter around the herbs and garlic to coat them.

After 2 minutes of searing on the other side, place the whole pan in the oven and bake for 8 to 10 minutes until the steaks reach 145°F (63°C) or your desired doneness. Let the steaks rest for 5 minutes before serving, so the juices can settle back into the meat. Remove the toothpicks before serving.

These steaks are great served alongside the Brown Sugar and Harissa Glazed Carrots (page 98).

Quick-Simmered Chicken in Yellow Curry

You don't have to wait hours for good flavors to develop in this quick-simmering yellow curry sauce. The combination of yellow curry and coconut milk makes for a creamy base to braise your chicken in. Served over rice, it becomes a full meal in a hurry.

SERVES: 4

2 tbsp (30 ml) olive oil

1 small sweet onion, finely chopped

1 lb (450 g) boneless, skinless chicken breast, cubed

Salt and pepper

2 tsp (4 g) fresh grated ginger

¼ tsp ground coriander

½ tsp turmeric

2 tbsp (30 g) yellow curry paste

1 (14-oz [414-ml]) can coconut milk

½ cup (118 ml) chicken broth

2 tsp (10 ml) fish sauce

½ lb (226 g) baby potatoes, cut in half

2 tbsp (3 g) cilantro or basil, minced

2 cups (400 g) rice, prepared

In your skillet over medium-low heat, add the olive oil. When the oil is shimmering and the pan is hot, add the onion and sauté for about 5 minutes, stirring frequently. Season the chicken with salt and pepper. Add the chicken to the pan and brown with the onions, about 5 to 6 minutes. Add the grated ginger, coriander, turmeric and yellow curry paste. Toss the chicken and the spices together. Whisk in the coconut milk, chicken broth and fish sauce until smooth. Add the cut potatoes, and bring the mixture to a simmer. Let the sauce thicken and the potatoes cook until they are tender, about 10 minutes. If the sauce is too thick or being absorbed too quickly, add more chicken broth to keep your desired consistency.

Simmer for 15 to 20 minutes until the chicken is cooked through and tender. Top with minced cilantro or basil for color and serve over rice. Try the Sesame, Lime and Cilantro Rice (page 105).

NOTE: Substitute red or green curry paste for this if you want to change things up. Omit the turmeric, if doing so.

Tandoori Chicken with Roasted Potatoes

Making tandoori chicken—yogurt-marinated chicken pan-fried until it's crispy on the outside and juicy on the inside—in the backyard isn't exactly an option for most people, but that's no reason to miss out on all the flavor that authentic tandoori can provide. Do double-duty by roasting your potatoes in the pan while your chicken marinates. Season your chicken with an extra dollop of creamy yogurt and minced cilantro to freshen things up.

SERVES: 4

1½ lb (680 g) baby red potatoes, diced

¼ cup + 3 tbsp (105 ml) extra-light olive oil, divided

½ tsp salt

½ tsp ground pepper

¾ cup (150 g) plain Greek yogurt

3–4 tbsp (15–20 g) tandoori spice blend

1 tsp (5 g) salt

½ tsp ground pepper

1½ tsp (3 g) fresh ground ginger

2 cloves garlic, minced

2 tbsp (30 g) tomato paste

1½ lb (680 g) chicken breast cutlets, thinly sliced

Yogurt, for serving

Cilantro, for serving

Preheat your oven to 425°F (220°C). While the oven is preheating, place the potatoes into the skillet. Drizzle 2 tablespoons (30 ml) olive oil over the potatoes and season with salt and pepper. Place the skillet into the oven and roast the potatoes for 20 minutes, stirring every 5 minutes to make sure that all the sides of the potatoes have roasted. Test the potatoes after 15 minutes to make sure they are cooking, and remove if they are fork-tender.

While the potatoes are roasting, pour the Greek yogurt, ¼ cup (60 ml) olive oil, tandoori spice blend, salt, pepper, ginger, garlic and tomato paste into a zip-top plastic bag. Gently squish the bag to combine the ingredients. You can also whisk the ingredients together beforehand if you wish, and pour them into the bag. Place the chicken cutlets into the bag, seal it and marinate the chicken for at least 20 minutes. You can also make this a couple of hours in advance and allow the chicken to marinate longer.

Once the potatoes are done, remove them from the skillet and set them aside on a plate that has been tented with foil. Scrape away any bits of potato that may be stuck to the pan. Add an additional tablespoon (15 ml) of extra-light olive oil to the pan and swirl to coat the bottom. Heat the skillet over medium-high heat until the olive oil is just shimmering on the bottom. Remove each chicken breast slice from the bag, allowing it to drip away most of the marinade. Place each cutlet into the pan, with the thickest part closest to the middle. Sear the chicken cutlets for approximately 5 minutes per side. Do not check them often or they will not crisp appropriately.

Once they are done and have reached at least 165°F (75°C), remove them from the pan and place them on the plate with the potatoes, tenting the plate again to allow the chicken to rest for 5 minutes. Serve with potatoes, yogurt and cilantro on top.

NOTE: You can also use garam masala for a twist or pork tenderloin as a change, if you don't want to use chicken.

5 Ingredients or Less

Far too frequently recipes call for obscure ingredients or just a minuscule amount of a single spice, neither of which you will likely use again. Still, you don't throw it out just in case you will need it a year down the road. This is basically my life story. And when you are an apartment dweller with little space in the kitchen, keeping all these extra ingredients is difficult. This chapter sets its sights on flavor-packed recipes that don't leave you overloaded with useless fluff you can't use again. We highlight five ingredients that will make each dish shine. Simple ingredients like salt, pepper or garlic don't count toward the final five ingredients list.

The Banh Mi Skillet Meatballs (page 97) give you the savory freshness of a true banh mi without compiling five bottles of oils, vinegars, sauces and syrups together to achieve it. The Brown Sugar and Harissa Glazed Carrots (page 98) are sweet and tangy and simple enough for a weeknight side dish with the must-have roasted red pepper harissa sauce. And the Three Mushroom and Goat Cheese Crostata (page 87), with sautéed mushrooms and crumbled goat cheese all wrapped in a flaky pie crust, is great as a meal for two or sliced up as a party appetizer.

Nutella-Strawberry Panini

My grandma introduced me to Nutella at a very young age, and it has been a fixture in my life ever since. This panini is the perfect dessert for chocolate and strawberry lovers, with crispy toasted sweetened bread, warm melted Nutella and sweet summer strawberries all mixed together. Make this for dessert with an optional scoop of ice cream on top. Who are we kidding? The ice cream is mandatory.

SERVES: 2

1 cup (280 g) Nutella

4 (1-inch [3-cm]) thick slices of French bread

2 cups (360 g) sliced fresh strawberries

2 tbsp (28 g) butter

2 tbsp (16 g) powdered sugar

1 cup (152 g) vanilla ice cream

Preheat your cast-iron skillet over medium-low heat. Divide the Nutella among the slices of French bread, spreading evenly.

Lay the strawberries evenly over the Nutella. Sandwich together to make 2 sandwiches.

Melt the butter in a skillet, swirling the butter to coat the pan. Place each sandwich into the pan, and coat the outer side of the bread with butter. Immediately flip each sandwich and coat the other side with any remaining butter in the pan. Cook the sandwiches until golden brown, about 4 minutes per side.

Slice in half, sprinkle with powdered sugar, and top each sandwich with vanilla ice cream. Serve immediately.

Three Mushroom and Goat Cheese Crostata

For an easy-to-prepare appetizer that is fit for fall, you can't overlook the simple elegance of a crostata. Typically sweet, this crostata with sautéed mushrooms can be perfectly placed at your next happy-hour or wine-tasting event, and it is wonderfully set for a quick weeknight vegetarian meal for two. If you go the meal route, I highly suggest adding an egg on top. Because everything is better with an egg on top.

SERVES: 8

2 tbsp (27 g) salted butter, divided

1 lb (450 g) mushrooms, chanterelle, cremini, button or other, trimmed and uniformly cut into pieces

Salt and pepper

1 tsp (1 g) fresh thyme, minced

½ cup (75 g) goat cheese

1 packaged pie crust, thawed and rolled out

1 egg (optional)

Preheat your oven to 425°F (220°C).

In your skillet over medium heat, add 1 tablespoon (15 g) of the butter and melt until simmering. Add half the mushrooms at a time so they cook evenly. Sauté so they soften and release their liquid, and then allow the liquid to evaporate, about 5 to 10 minutes a batch. Stir in salt, pepper and half the thyme. Set the cooked mushrooms aside in a bowl and repeat with the other half of the mushrooms and the remaining butter. Add the second batch to the bowl as well. Wipe the skillet clean, and remove it from the heat.

Sprinkle half of the goat cheese onto the middle of the rolled-out pie crust, and pile the mushrooms over the top. Gently fold the edges of the crust over itself to contain the mushrooms.

In a small dish, whisk together the egg and 1 tablespoon (15 ml) of cool water to form an egg wash. Brush it over the crust's edges and transfer the crostata to the warm skillet. Bake for 25 to 30 minutes until the crust is golden brown. Remove the crostata from the oven, and sprinkle the remaining half of the goat cheese over the top of the mushrooms. Let the crostata rest for 5 minutes before slicing and serving.

NOTE: Use mushrooms that are in season wherever you are to mix and match flavors.

Chicken-and-Apple Sausage and Swiss Chard Skillet

We are always trying to find ways to incorporate more greens into our diet. This skillet is done in record time. Swiss chard is a wonderful switch from standard spinach, keeping a little tooth to it even when wilted. And using premade chicken sausages readily available at the store means this is one dinner than can be made in a hurry without sacrificing flavor or time. The chicken-and-apple sausages lend a subtle sweetness to the dish, with the cannellini beans creating a buttery texture when fried.

SERVES: 4

2 tbsp (30 ml) olive oil, divided

1 (12-oz [340-g]) package premade chicken-and-apple sausage, sliced on the bias

1 lb (450 g) Swiss chard, ribs cut away, roughly chopped

1 (15-oz [425-g]) can cannellini or navy beans, drained and rinsed

2 cloves garlic, minced

Salt and pepper

Heat your skillet over medium heat and add 1 tablespoon (15 ml) of olive oil. When the oil is shimmering and heated up, add the sausage slices and sauté until crispy and brown on each side, about 3 minutes per side. Remove them from the skillet onto a spare plate. Add the other tablespoon (15 ml) of the olive oil to the skillet. Sauté the Swiss chard in two batches until it is wilted, about 4 minutes per batch. Set aside onto the same plate as the cooked sausages. Lastly, add the beans and heat through, about 2 minutes. Add the sausage and Swiss chard to the beans, tossing to combine all the ingredients. Serve immediately.

NOTE: Use any flavored sausage you choose, since each flavor will change this dish slightly every time.

Caprese Omelet

Some of the best things about summer are the evenings spent on the patio with friends, drinking wine and eating fresh caprese from the tomatoes right out of your garden. But the more ways you can consume tomatoes and basil, the better. This simple omelet really gets the summer treatment with just a few everyday ingredients.

SERVES: 1 to 2

4 eggs

2 tbsp (29 g) butter

Salt and pepper

¼ cup (28 g) shredded mozzarella

1 cup (250 g) cherry tomatoes, halved and quartered, depending on size

5–6 basil leaves, chiffonade

In a mixing bowl, thoroughly whisk the eggs until light and fluffy. In your well-seasoned skillet over medium heat, add the butter and allow it to melt until simmering. Swirl the pan to make sure the whole bottom is coated. Pour the whisked eggs into the pan and allow the eggs to begin to set. While they set, season with salt and pepper. If bubbles pop up, tamp them down with a spatula. The eggs should set in about 3 to 4 minutes. When the top of the eggs is just getting ready to set, add the mozzarella, tomatoes and basil to one half of the eggs. Using a spatula, gently turn over the other half of the eggs to create your omelet.

Once the eggs are totally set, plate the omelet. Add any remaining tomatoes, basil or cheese. Devour immediately.

Dutch Babies for One (or More)

Dutch babies are the perfect blend of pancake and crêpe for those mornings you can't decide which you're craving more. This recipe was given to me by one of my best friends, and I've put it to use countless times in my own kitchen ever since. The predictable ratio of ingredients makes this one an easy recipe to make for one or for a crowd. Here we have it serving two, but you can halve it for one or double the ingredients below to serve four.

SERVES: 2

½ cup (60 g) flour

½ cup (120 ml) milk

¼ cup (50 g) sugar

2 eggs

½ tsp vanilla

2 tbsp (30 g) butter

½ cup (75 g) strawberries (optional)

½ cup (115 g) sliced bananas (optional)

¼ cup (60 ml) maple syrup (optional)

Preheat your oven to 400°F (205°C).

In your mixing bowl, add all the ingredients except for the fruit and maple syrup and whisk thoroughly until the mix is smooth. Set the Dutch baby batter aside. Preheat two skillets over medium heat. Spray your skillets with nonstick spray or melt in some butter. If using butter, make sure that the butter is simmering slightly before adding the Dutch baby batter.

Divide the batter between the two skillets and immediately place them in your preheated oven. Bake for 12 to 15 minutes or until the Dutch babies are golden brown. Remove them from the oven and serve immediately. They will deflate once they are removed from the oven, but that is normal. The edges are like a pancake and the middle is like a crepe. Enjoy the best of both worlds!

Serve this with fresh fruit on top or with syrup for the purists.

Ginger Teriyaki, Beef, Broccoli and Bok Choy

This is one of the recipes you will keep in your back pocket on those days that you, as the hipsters say, "can't even." Oh, wait—I'm one of those people who says that. Flank steak is quick to prepare and isn't fussy. The bok choy and broccoli stay slightly crunchy with a quick sauté, making this your new favorite way to do takeout. It's take*in*. Marinate your sliced flank steak the night before to infuse it with teriyaki and fresh ginger. If marinating the night before can't be done, 30 minutes to 1 hour will do.

SERVES: 4

1 head broccoli

3–4 heads baby bok choy

1½ lb (680 g) flank steak, sliced thinly against the grain

1 cup (240 ml) low-sodium teriyaki sauce

1–1½ tbsp (8–12 g) grated ginger

Prepare the broccoli by using a sharp knife and cutting away the florets. Slice any stems left over into strips. Don't throw them away. Next, prepare the bok choy, cutting off the bottom enough to separate the leaves. Peel away the leaves of the bok choy, and slice any particularly large leaves in half lengthwise. Set all the vegetables aside.

In your skillet over medium-high heat, add the flank steak and sear until crispy, about 1 to 2 minutes. Flip the steak over and continue to sear until all sides are crispy, another 1 to 2 minutes. If you like your beef rare, sear it for less time. Remove the steak and place it on a plate. In the skillet, pour in all the veggies and toss with teriyaki sauce. Add the ginger and sauté the veggies until they are nearly softened, about 5 minutes. Add the steak back into the pan and toss with the vegetables to combine. Finish steaming the vegetables until they are fork-tender. Serve immediately next to some Sesame, Lime and Cilantro Rice (page 105).

Banh Mi Skillet Meatballs

There is something so fresh and fun about banh mi and its mix of fresh vegetables and herbs with totally kicking pork. This skillet simplifies things without sacrificing flavor. When cravings for Thai food strike and you can't bear to go out, you can go with what you have on hand. Add banh mi dumplings or eat it straight from the skillet. Not that I would know what that is like . . . shhh.

SERVES: 4

1 (1½-lb [680-g]) package of 28 pork meatballs

½ cup (120 ml) sweet chili sauce

¼ cup (60 ml) low-sodium teriyaki sauce

1 tbsp (15 ml) fish sauce (optional)

1 cup (110 g) shredded carrot

¼ cup (4 g) minced cilantro

¼ cup (23 g) thinly sliced jalapeño

Preheat your skillet over medium heat. Add your package of premade pork meatballs. After about 3 minutes, add the sweet chili sauce and low-sodium teriyaki sauce and toss the meatballs until they are coated. If you are using fish sauce, add it during this step, too. Fish sauce adds a more authentic flavor, but it's also one more bottle to store in your fridge, so I get it if it isn't your speed.

Cover the meatballs and let them cook, stirring them every few minutes to ensure they are heated through.

Once the meatballs reach 165°F (75°F C), turn off the heat on the stove and remove your skillet. Pour the carrots, cilantro and jalapeño on top and serve immediately.

NOTE: If you can't find premade pork meatballs in your grocery store, substitute plain beef meatballs.

Brown Sugar and Harissa Glazed Carrots

These are not your usual eye rollingly predictable carrots. Red pepper harissa and brown sugar are the perfect combination of sweet and hot for your everyday dinner or for holidays! Add cilantro just before serving for a fresh twist and pop of color.

SERVES: 4

2 tbsp (30 g) butter

2 lb (907 g) carrots, peeled and sliced on the bias

¼ tsp salt

¼ cup (50 g) brown sugar, more or less to your taste

2–3 tbsp (30–45 ml) harissa

Heat your skillet over medium heat. Add the butter and allow it to melt. Once the butter starts to simmer, add the carrots, stirring them to coat them in the butter. Turn the heat down to medium low. Gently salt and allow the carrots to sauté until they begin to turn golden brown, about 5 to 7 minutes. Continue to sauté the carrots on the other side for another 5 to 7 minutes or until the carrots are nearly tender enough to put a fork through. Add the brown sugar and toss the carrots to coat them evenly. Continue to sauté until the sugar begins to caramelize, about 4 to 5 minutes. Once the brown sugar caramelizes, add the harissa and coat the carrots.

Once they are mixed, serve them immediately.

Sausage-and-Gruyère-Stuffed Onions

Crispy pork sausage and Gruyère cheese give this humble dish a kick in the elevated direction. The flavors meld in the comfort of hollowed-out sweet onions, giving this five-ingredient dish a real depth of flavor. Make these ahead of time and bake them when you're ready.

SERVES: 4

12 oz (340 g) pork sausage (I use a sage variety.)

4 sweet onions, evenly sized

½ cup (30 g) panko bread crumbs

1 cup (100 g) Gruyère cheese or other sharp cheese

1½ cups (350 ml) chicken broth

Preheat your oven to 425°F (220°C).

Place your skillet over medium-high heat, and add the pork sausage, breaking it apart with a wooden spoon until crispy and cooked through, about 10 minutes. While you are browning the sausage, cut off the top quarter of each onion, and use a melon baller to scoop each one out, reserving the insides for the stuffing.

Cut off the bottom of the onion to create a flat face to keep the stuffed onions upright while roasting. Take the leftover insides of the onions, chop them finely and add them to the crispy sausage. Continue to cook until the onions have softened, about 4 to 5 minutes. Then sprinkle in the panko bread crumbs and Gruyère cheese and mix them into the sausage and onion stuffing. Next, stuff the onions with the sausage stuffing and place them back in the skillet. If there is extra stuffing left in the pan that is okay. Pour the chicken broth into the pan and cover it with aluminum foil.

Bake the onions for 35 minutes or until they're soft when they're poked with a sharp knife. Top the onions with any remaining stuffing and sauce left in the pan. Serve immediately.

NOTE: Use an Italian- or sage-flavored pork sausage to add flavor without adding extra ingredients.

Ginger-Shallot Salmon Patties

Fresh salmon in the summer is one of life's great joys, and we devour it with reckless abandon here in the Pacific Northwest. This salmon recipe uses fresh minced ginger and shallots, which give it an Asian-inspired flair with minimal ingredients.

SERVES: 4

1½ lb (680 g) skinless and deboned salmon filets, finely chopped

3 tbsp (23 g) minced shallots

2 tbsp (16 g) grated fresh ginger

1 egg, beaten

½ tsp red pepper flakes

Salt and pepper

3 tbsp (45 ml) vegetable oil

1 tbsp (15 ml) lime juice, optional

2 tbsp (6 g) chopped cilantro, optional

In a mixing bowl, mix together the finely chopped salmon, shallots, ginger, egg and red pepper flakes. Season the mix with salt and pepper. Divide the salmon into 8 patties and place them on a parchment-lined baking sheet. Freeze the patties for at least 20 minutes.

While the patties are freezing, heat up your skillet over medium-high heat and add vegetable oil. When the oil is shimmering, it will be ready for the patties. Add 4 patties at a time to allow enough space between them. Fry on each side until deep golden brown, approximately 5 minutes per side.

Spritz with lime juice and cilantro to serve if the mood strikes you!

NOTE: Add sesame seeds to the mixture if you have them on hand for a light, nutty flavor.

Sesame, Lime and Cilantro Rice

Rice can be a ubiquitous addition to a meal, but punching it up with toasted sesame oil, fresh lime and cilantro helps it hold its own next to any main dish. This is a wonderful complement to the Ginger-Shallot Salmon Patties (page 102).

SERVES: 4

1 cup (185 g) long grain rice

1½ cups (350 ml) water

Salt and pepper

½ tsp toasted sesame oil

½ tsp lime zest

2 tbsp (6 g) minced cilantro

In your Dutch oven, bring the rice and water to a boil, seasoning the water with salt and pepper. Reduce the water to a simmer, and cook until the rice is tender and the water is fully absorbed, about 15 to 18 minutes. Remove the Dutch oven from the stove and, using a large spoon, stir in the toasted sesame oil, lime zest and cilantro. Toss the rice to combine all the ingredients and serve immediately.

NOTE: Swap the rice for quinoa for a change in grains.

Quick and Simple Beef Stew

Beef stew is the epitome of comfort food. Sometimes you just want to throw whatever you have on hand into a pan and let it go. There are certain steps you need to get all those rich flavors, even if you don't have everything you need on hand. A couple of tips and tricks have saved me time and tears in the kitchen when all I wanted was soup and couldn't bear another trip to the store. I don't count oil as an ingredient here because it's an agent to the cooking.

SERVES: 6

2 lb (907 g) cubed chuck steak, cut into 1½-inch (4-cm) cubes

Salt and pepper

3 tbsp (45 ml) vegetable oil

4 cups (560 g) roughly chopped mirepoix (frozen carrot, onion, celery blend)

2 cups (475 ml) chicken or beef broth

1 cup (240 ml) red wine

1 lb (452 g) baby potatoes or root vegetables such as parsnips

Preheat your oven to 300°F (150°C) with the oven rack on the lower middle rack.

Pat the cubed beef dry with wads of paper towels. Season the beef liberally with salt and pepper. Heat the vegetable oil in the Dutch oven over medium-high heat. Working in batches, brown the chuck steak on all sides, about 2 to 3 minutes per side. Don't rush the browning process or pull the steak away from the pan if it has not naturally released on its own. Let the beef tell you when it's ready to flip. Moving it early will risk pulling away the seasoned beef and leaving it in the pan. Once the beef is done, put it on a plate to the side and repeat the browning with the rest of the steak.

Next, add the frozen mirepoix, stirring it in the pan to sweat and soften the vegetables for about 7 to 8 minutes. This will also deglaze the pan, pulling up some of those developed flavored bits baked into the bottom.

Stir in the broth and scrape the bottom of the pan to remove any other cooked-on food. Whisk in the red wine and add the beef back into the pan. Cover the Dutch oven and place it into the oven for 1 hour. When the hour is up, remove the lid and stir in the baby potatoes. Cover and continue to cook for 1 more hour.

Test the beef by pulling it apart with two forks. If there is resistance, continue to cook for another 20 to 30 minutes or until the beef falls apart easily.

NOTE: Keep frozen mirepoix on hand in your freezer. Equal parts carrots, celery and onion all frozen in 2 cup (280 g) portions will save you time and freak-outs when you just want stew!

Artisanal Carbs

Carbs are the staple of life—my life, anyway. There was never a meal made worse because of bread—unless it was my mother's biscuits, but that's another story. Baking bread can be intimidating, with fails, tears and tantrums along the way. But when your first successful loaf comes out of the oven, all the effort and trials will be vindicated, and you will have a skill for life.

Let's walk together step-by-step, making the Sweet Potato Dinner Rolls with Honey Butter (page 119), which are slightly sweet and herby with honey butter melting into every crack and sea salt delicately sprinkled on top. And the Apricot-Almond Babka (page 112) lets you practice your bread braiding to create a decorative wreath design that will steal the show on the holiday dessert table. It is in your power to do it, and I know you can.

Apple Cider Croissant Doughnuts

Food trends come and go just as quickly as your weekly grocery circular or acid-washed jeans or tube tops (thank goodness). But one I hope will stick around a little longer is the croissant doughnut. Croissants and doughnuts stand on their own as pillars of the carb universe, but mashing them together creates a cosmic explosion of butter and carbs that cannot be denied. Flaky, buttery, layered dough deep-fried and tossed in apple pie spice is the stuff dreams are made of.

SERVES: 12

¾ cup (180 ml) apple cider, warmed to approximately 100°F (38°C)

2¼ tsp (7 g) dry yeast

2 large eggs

1⅓ cup (260 g) sugar, divided

2 tsp (10 ml) vanilla paste, divided

2½ tsp (8 g) apple pie spice, divided

3½ cups (420 g) all-purpose flour, divided

1 tsp (5 g) salt

2 sticks butter, at room temperature

1 qt (950 ml) vegetable oil, for frying

NOTE: Omit the apple cider and substitute it for buttermilk if you want a tangy flavor.

In your mixing bowl, stir together the apple cider and yeast and allow the yeast to proof for about 5 minutes until it becomes frothy. If your yeast does not become frothy, toss it out and start with fresh yeast. Once the mixture is frothy, stir in the eggs, ⅓ cup (60 g) sugar, 1 teaspoon (5 ml) vanilla paste and 1½ teaspoons (3 g) apple pie spice. Mix in 1 cup (120 g) of the flour and the salt. With your mixer on low, gradually add 2¼ cups (270 g) of flour. The last ¼ cup (30 g) of flour will be used later.

Continue to stir and knead the dough until it becomes smooth and elastic but remains a little tacky to the touch, about 5 to 7 minutes. Transfer the dough to a lightly greased mixing bowl, cover it with plastic wrap and allow it to rise for about 1 hour.

While the dough is rising, beat together the softened butter, remaining vanilla paste and last ¼ cup (30 g) of flour. Set it aside.

After the dough has risen, roll it out on a lightly floured surface into a 12 × 18-inch (30.5 × 46-cm) rectangle, about ¼ inch (0.5 cm) thick. Spread the vanilla butter evenly over the entire rectangle. Gently fold the dough over onto itself into thirds. Place it on a parchment-lined baking sheet, and cover it with plastic wrap. Place the dough in the fridge for 1 hour to chill and slow the rising process. Repeat this process two more times, rolling out the dough into a 12 x 18-inch (30.5 x 46-cm) rectangle, and folding it over a total of three times. After the third time, the dough should be 1 inch (2.5 cm) thick.

Use a doughnut cutter to cut out 12 doughnuts. Reroll the dough if needed. Place the doughnuts into the fridge to keep chilled while you heat up the vegetable oil to about 350°F (176°C) in your enameled Dutch oven.

Place a couple of doughnuts and doughnut holes at a time into the oil so as not to overcrowd them. Let them fry on one side until they are golden brown, about 3 to 4 minutes. Gently flip and repeat. Remove them from the oil and let them drain on a baking sheet lined with several paper towels. Once the doughnuts are done, combine the remaining 1 cup (200 g) of sugar and 1 teaspoon (5 g) of apple pie spice. Toss each of the doughnuts and doughnut holes into the sugar and serve immediately.

Apricot-Almond Babka

Every once in a while you need to change things up. Chocolate seems to be the usual filling for babka these days, but instead, let's take time to appreciate the wonderful sweetness of apricot and marzipan together. Baking this in a skillet instead of in the traditional loaf pan creates a beautiful, wreath-like effect that will wow during the holidays!

SERVES: 8

2¼ tsp (7 g) dry yeast

1 tbsp (12 g) sugar

½ cup (120 ml) milk, warmed

6 tbsp (90 g) unsalted butter, melted and cooled

1 egg, lightly beaten

¼ tsp salt

2–2¼ cups (240–280 g) flour

½ cup (160 g) apricot preserves, gently warmed to make it soft to spread

¼ cup (65 g) almond paste (marzipan), flaked

½ cup (100 g) sugar

½ cup (120 ml) water

NOTE: Use other jams in lieu of apricot to see what your favorite combination is!

In the bowl of a stand mixer, gently mix together the yeast, sugar and warm milk. Let the yeast proof for at least 5 minutes, until the yeast becomes foamy on top and activates. Stir in the butter, egg and salt. With the mixer outfitted with a hook attachment, slowly add 2 cups (240 g) of the flour until it is all incorporated. Turn the mixer to medium, and knead the dough until it is smooth and elastic, about 5 minutes. The dough should pull away from the sides of the bowl. If it does not, return the mixer to low speed and add the remaining ¼ cup (30 g) of flour 1 tablespoon (8 g) at a time until the dough pulls away from the sides. It should still be stuck to the bottom of the mixing bowl. That is okay.

If time is on your side, cover the bowl and place it in the fridge overnight to slow the rising process and "age" the dough. This will develop a more complex flavor. If you are unable to do that, cover the bowl and allow the dough to rise for at least 1 hour on your countertop. Once it has doubled in size, you are ready for the next step.

On a lightly floured countertop or surface, turn out the dough and roll it into a rectangle, about 12 × 18 inches (30 × 45 cm). If the dough is difficult to roll, let it rest a few minutes. Spread the apricot preserves over the dough. Using a fork, gently flake the almond paste over the top of the apricot jam.

Using both hands, roll the long edge of the dough tightly around to create a log. Pinch the seams of the dough closed. With a sharp knife, slice the dough lengthwise in half so you can see the inside.

To form the dough wreath, overlap the two strips of dough to create a twist, working your way down the dough until you reach the other end. Bring the two ends together and gently pinch them together to form a wreath. Transfer the wreath to the nonstick-sprayed or parchment-lined skillet and allow it to rise for an additional hour before baking.

Preheat your oven to 375°F (190°C), and bake the babka for approximately 30 minutes. While the babka is baking, make a simple syrup by combining the sugar and water in a saucepan and bringing it to a boil. When the mixture has boiled and the sugar is dissolved, set it aside and brush it over the babka when it comes out of the oven. Allow the babka to cool completely before serving.

Green Chili and Cheddar Beer Bread

Pairing splendidly with a hearty soup in winter, beer bread is a true complement to a warming meal. Mix your fillings to match whatever soup you are craving. This green chili and cheddar corn bread holds its own next to a piping hot bowl of white chicken chili.

SERVES: 6 to 8

2½ cups (300 g) flour

2 tbsp (25 g) sugar

1 tbsp (11 g) baking powder

1 tsp (5 g) salt

½ tsp ground pepper

2 cups (226 g) shredded cheddar, divided

1 (4-oz [113-g]) can mild chopped green chilies

6 tbsp (85) butter

12 oz (350 ml) Mexican beer

Preheat your oven to 375°F (190°C).

In a large bowl, whisk together the flour, sugar, baking powder, salt and pepper. Stir in 1½ cups (170 g) of the cheddar cheese and the green chilies until they are combined, breaking up any clumps of cheese.

Heat your cast-iron skillet on the stove over medium heat. Add the butter to the skillet and melt it, swirling it around until the bottom and sides of the skillet are coated. Drizzle the melted butter over the dry ingredients, and set aside the skillet. This eliminates having to grease the pan or get another dish dirty melting butter in the microwave.

Pour the beer over the rest of the bread ingredients and stir until just combined. Be sure not to overmix the bread; it's supposed to be lumpy and very thick.

Pour the bread batter into the heated skillet and spread it out over the whole pan. Sprinkle with the remaining cheddar cheese. Bake immediately for 15 to 20 minutes or until a toothpick inserted into the middle comes out clean. Remove the skillet from the oven and let cool slightly before slicing and serving.

Rosemary and Roasted Garlic Focaccia

One of my favorite memories as a kid is the pressed sandwiches my mom used to make for road trips and picnics. The sandwiches were packed with salamis, roast beef, cheeses, olive tapenades, red onion and more, and encased in fluffy herbed focaccia. And here I am making them again now that this recipe is in our home. The rosemary and roasted garlic mixed into the fluffy dough and dappled with kalamata olives is the perfect bread for sandwiches or as an accompaniment to soup or any favorite meal. If you are new to bread baking, let this be your first—it's simple enough for beginners and a staple for experts.

SERVES: 12

1½ cups (360 ml) warm water

2 tsp (10 ml) honey

2¼ tsp (7 g) dry active yeast

3 tbsp (45 ml) olive oil plus extra for bowl and dish

1½ tsp (9 g) sea salt

6 cloves roasted garlic, smashed

2 tbsp (4 g) fresh minced rosemary

4 cups (480 g) all-purpose flour

¾ cup (106 g) pitted kalamata olives

Sea salt and pepper

In your stand mixer outfitted with a hook attachment, pour the warm water and honey and stir until the honey dissolves. Gently stir in the yeast, and let the yeast proof for about 5 to 10 minutes, until it is foamy on top. Stir in the 3 tablespoons (45 ml) of oil, salt, smashed roasted garlic and fresh minced rosemary. Next, turn the mixer on low and slowly add the flour. Knead into a dough with the mixer on low for about 10 minutes. The dough should pull away from the sides of the bowl but still remain stuck to the bottom. If the dough is not pulling away from the sides, add an additional ¼ cup (30 g) of flour, 1 tablespoon (8 g) at a time, until it does.

Remove the dough hook and cover the bowl with plastic wrap, allowing the dough to rise for about 60 to 90 minutes, until it has doubled in size. Remove the plastic wrap and reinstall the dough hook. Turn the mixer back on for 30 seconds to tamp down the rise.

Spray your skillet with nonstick spray, and turn the dough out into the skillet. Gently spread the dough out toward the edges of the pan using your fingertips to leave indents in it. If the dough does not go out all the way to the edges of the pan that is okay; the second rise will take care of that. Push the olives into the dough as deep as possible to avoid them popping up as it rises. Drizzle the top with more olive oil and sprinkle with sea salt and pepper. Cover the dough with a clean, damp towel. Allow the dough to rise again for another hour.

Preheat your oven to 400°F (205°C). Bake for 30 to 35 minutes, or until the dough looks slightly crispy on top. Place the skillet on a wire rack to cool completely. Slice and serve.

Sweet Potato Dinner Rolls with Honey Butter

Quite possibly the fluffiest roll you will ever have, these dinner rolls disappear from the table in an instant thanks to their sweet flavor, light texture and melted honey butter on top. Sprinkle them with sea salt and prepare to be amazed. For beginning bread makers, this is a great first bread-baking recipe. It uses leftover mashed sweet potatoes for color and flavor, but you can use white potatoes as well if you wish. If you are making these for a crowd, this recipe can easily be doubled.

SERVES: 8 to 10

2 tbsp (30 ml) milk

¼ cup (60 ml) water

1 tsp + 2 tbsp (30 g) sugar, divided

1¼ tsp (4 g) yeast

1 egg

¼ tsp salt

3 tbsp (45 g) butter, melted and cooled

½ cup (125 g) mashed sweet potato

2¼–2½ cups (270–300 g) all-purpose flour, more depending on moisture of dough

¼ cup (60 g) butter, room temperature

2 tbsp (30 ml) honey

Sea salt

NOTE: Freeze the rolls once they are shaped so you can heat and serve them when the craving strikes.

In a small bowl or measuring cup, combine the milk and water. Heat in a microwave until the temperature reaches between 102°F (39°C) and 110°F (43°C), about 40 seconds. Stir 1 teaspoon (5 g) of sugar into the mixture and add the yeast. Gently mix in the yeast, and set aside to allow the yeast to activate and become foamy, about 5 minutes.

With a stand mixer fitted with the dough hook attachment, add in the egg, salt, 3 tablespoons (45 g) butter, sweet potato and flour and mix until combined, about 2 minutes. Slowly pour in the yeast mixture, and allow it to incorporate. Mix until the ingredients are smooth and doughlike, and the dough pulls away from the sides of the bowl but still sticks to the bottom. This will take about 8 minutes. If the dough is still sticking to the sides of the bowl after 8 minutes, add an additional ¼ cup (30 g) of flour, 1 tablespoon (8 g) at a time, until the dough releases from the sides.

Roll the dough out onto a lightly floured surface. Knead the dough until it becomes a smooth, uniform ball. Place it into a lightly greased bowl, cover it with plastic wrap and set it in a warm place for about 1 hour or until the dough doubles in size.

Roll the dough out onto a lightly floured surface, and cut it into 8 to 10 equal pieces. Roll the dough into small balls, and place them seam-side down in a greased skillet. Cover and let the dough rise until the rolls have doubled in size, about 1 hour.

Preheat your oven to 350°F (176°C). Bake for 20 to 25 minutes or until the rolls are golden brown on top and have reached 200°F (94°C) when tested with a thermometer.

In a small dish, mix together ¼ cup (60 g) room-temperature butter and 2 tablespoons (30 ml) honey until smooth. Brush the tops of the baked rolls with this mixture, sprinkle with sea salt and serve warm.

Applesauce and Raisin Skillet Cake

Something about snack cakes makes them perfect for any occasion—dessert, after-school snack, or, dare I say, breakfast? Such a rebel. This sweet and hearty-but-tender cake is good for everything. It's sweetened with apple sauce and golden raisins, meaning you can use less refined sugar all while keeping it tender and moist. The applesauce and cider give this a nice apple flavor, accentuated by the apple pie spice, without going over the top. My in-laws brought Ben and me a gallon of applesauce while I was writing this book, and it led to many happy batches of this cake. I hope you will get as much use out of applesauce as we did. And just as much joy.

SERVES: 12

1 cup (240 ml) apple cider

1 cup (150 g) golden raisins or dried apples

1½ cups (180 g) flour

1 tsp (4 g) baking soda

⅔ cup (132 g) sugar, divided

1 tsp (5 g) apple pie spice

1 egg

½ tsp salt

½ cup (120 g) unsalted butter, melted and cooled

1 tsp (5 ml) vanilla extract

1 cup (246 g) applesauce

Preheat your oven to 350°F (176°C).

If you are not using a well-seasoned skillet, line your skillet bottom with a round of parchment paper. In a small saucepan, add the apple cider and the raisins or dried apples. Bring them to a simmer and let the fruit absorb the cider. Turn the heat off after about 5 minutes, or when they start simmering, and let them cool in the pan.

While the fruit is cooling, whisk together the flour and baking soda. In another bowl, whisk together the sugar and apple pie spice. Set aside 2 tablespoons (25 g) of the sugar mixture for later to top the cake. In the mixing bowl, whisk in the egg, salt, melted and cooled butter and vanilla. Whisk together until light and fluffy, about 30 seconds. In your food processor, blend together the cider-and-raisin mixture until nearly smooth. Fold the applesauce into the egg-and-butter mixture until it's completely combined. Lastly, fold in the flour mixture until just incorporated. Pour into the lined skillet, and smooth with the back of a spoon or spatula. Sprinkle the remaining apple pie spice sugar over the top of the cake and place it in the oven for about 35 minutes, checking at 30 minutes just to be sure it's not overcooking. Test the doneness with a toothpick in the middle of the pan. If a few crumbs remain on the toothpick, it is ready to remove from the oven.

Place it on a wire rack to cool completely before serving.

Butterscotch and Butternut Pancakes

As much as I look forward to fall for ushering in sweater season and all things pumpkin, I don't want to forget about all of the other squashes that are versatile in so many ways. This recipe is great for any variety of creamy squashes, like acorn, or even try sweet potato! Add pecans to the mixture before cooking for a crunchy fall texture.

SERVES: 16

1⅓ cups (160 g) all-purpose flour

¼ cup (40 g) corn meal

¼ cup (47 g) brown sugar

2 tsp (10 g) baking powder

½ tsp salt

2 tsp (3 g) pumpkin pie spice

2 eggs

1¼–1½ cups (300–360 ml) milk

½ cup (225 g) butternut squash puree

2 tbsp (15 ml) vegetable oil

½ cup (120 g) butterscotch chips

In one mixing bowl, whisk together all of the dry ingredients except the butterscotch chips. In another mixing bowl, whisk together your eggs, milk, butternut squash puree and vegetable oil until uniformly mixed. Pour the egg mixture into the dry ingredients and, using a rubber spatula, fold the batter until just a couple of flour streaks remain. Lastly, mix in the butterscotch chips. The mixture will look slightly lumpy, but that is okay. Let the batter rest.

Spray your skillet with nonstick spray, and preheat it over medium-low heat. Once your skillet is preheated, pour enough batter into the pan to create a 4- to 5-inch (10- to 13-cm) circle. If there is too much batter, the pancakes may be spongy in the middle instead of fluffy. The pancakes should bubble in the middle and their edges should look dry before you flip them, about 3 minutes. Flip and then cook until they're golden brown on the bottom, another 3 minutes. Remove the pancakes from the skillet and plate into tall stacks! Serve with plenty of syrup.

NOTE: If you can't find butternut squash puree, substitute pumpkin puree in this recipe.

Deep-Dish Pizza Napoletana

In a world where we are told that more is better, sometimes we must relish simplicity—
it can be a beautiful thing. There are a few tips that make this pizza better than the takeout
we have become accustomed to. A preheated skillet is key to a crispy crust, replicating the effects
of a pizza stone. The addition of high-quality sauce and a smattering of mozzarella and fresh
basil keep this pizza as traditional as it gets without having to go to Italy to find it.

SERVES: 2 to 3

1 lb (453 g) premade pizza dough

10 fresh basil leaves

½ cup (120 ml) high-quality pizza sauce

½ cup (56 g) shredded mozzarella
(whole fat, low moisture)

Place your well-seasoned skillet into the oven, and preheat your oven to 450°F (230°C). This simple step is critical to getting your crust crispy. While the oven is preheating, take the pizza dough out of the refrigerator and allow it to rest on the counter for at least 20 minutes. While the dough is resting, rinse and dry your basil leaves.

After 20 minutes of rest, stretch the dough to 12 inches (30 cm) in diameter. Carefully remove the skillet from the oven, and carefully lay the dough on the bottom of the skillet, letting the edges come slightly up the sides of the skillet. Spread the pizza sauce around the dough, keeping the outer 1 inch (2.5 cm) sauce-free. Lay the basil leaves on top of the sauce, and then sprinkle with mozzarella. Place the pizza in the oven immediately and bake for 12 to 14 minutes, or until the cheese is bubbling and the crust is golden brown. Let the pizza rest for 5 minutes before slicing.

NOTE: Many store delis have premade dough. If you can't find it there, stop by your local pizza shop to see if they will sell it to you directly.

Gingerbread Coffee Cake

When the holidays hit, it's all hands on the gingerbread cookies. Gingerbread has always had a special place in my heart thanks to my grandmother's endless supply of frosted gingerbread cookies in her kitchen. So I decided to morph it into a coffee cake. Now you can start your frosty winter mornings curled up by the fire with a cup of coffee in one hand and a slice of this gingerbread coffee cake in another.

SERVES: 8

5 cubes (¼ cup [23 g]) candied ginger

¾ cup (150 g) sugar

2 cups (240 g) flour

2 tsp (10 g) baking powder

2½ tsp (7 g) ground cinnamon, divided

½ tsp ground ginger

½ tsp ground cloves

½ tsp ground nutmeg

½ tsp ground allspice

½ tsp salt

⅔ cup (160 ml) molasses

1½ tsp (8 ml) vanilla extract

2 eggs

½ cup (120 g) butter, melted and cooled

¾ cup (90 g) sour cream or plain yogurt

½ cup (100 g) white sugar

⅓ cup (90 g) brown sugar

⅓ cup (40 g) flour

4 tbsp (60 g) butter, chilled and cubed

½ cup (75 g) pecans, chopped

Preheat your oven to 350°F (176°C).

In a small food processor, add in the candied ginger and the white sugar. Pulse the food processor until the candied ginger is completely mixed into the sugar, about 5 pulses. Set it aside. Keep the food processor; you will need it for making the streusel later.

In a large bowl, whisk together the flour, baking powder, ½ teaspoon of cinnamon, the rest of the spices and salt. Set it aside. In another large bowl, whisk together the molasses, ginger-sugar blend, vanilla, eggs, butter and sour cream or yogurt until the mixture is totally smooth. Gently fold the wet mixture into the flour mixture just until there are a couple of white streaks left. Add the batter to a greased 10-inch (25-cm) skillet, and spread it out until it nearly touches the edges of the pan.

Back in the food processor, add in the white sugar, brown sugar, flour and remaining cinnamon. Pulse to mix them together. Add the butter cubes and the pecans, and pulse 5 to 8 times just until some crumbles form. Use your hands and create larger crumbles if needed.

Sprinkle the crumbles over the coffee cake, and place it in the oven for 25 to 30 minutes, or until a toothpick comes out clean. Immediately place the skillet on a cooling rack to avoid overbaking the cake. Cool completely, and then slice and serve.

Pesto-and-Mozzarella-Stuffed Dinner Rolls

Let's be honest, these will disappear from your table faster than crescent rolls out of the tube. Piping hot mozzarella cheese and fresh pesto ooze out of each roll from the first bite.

SERVES: 12 to 16

1¼ cups (300 ml) milk, warmed to 100°F–110°F (37°C–43°C)

½ cup (120 g) unsalted butter, melted and cooled

1 egg

4 cups (480 g) all-purpose flour

2 tbsp (25 g) sugar

2¼ tsp (7 g) instant yeast

2 tbsp (5 g) dried basil

1 tsp (5 g) salt

⅓ cup (80 ml) prepared pesto

8 oz (225 g) whole milk mozzarella, cut into 12–16 cubes

¼ cup (20 g) shredded Parmesan

In a bowl or large measuring cup, whisk together your warmed milk, butter and egg until combined. In the bowl of your stand mixer, stir together the flour, sugar, yeast, dried basil and salt. With the mixer on low, slowly pour in the milk mixture until it is completely added in, and continue mixing on low until the dough begins to come together, 2 to 3 minutes.

Next, turn the mixer onto medium, and knead the dough for about 6 to 7 minutes until the dough is smooth and elastic. The dough should be pulling away from the sides of the bowl, but the dough will still stick to the bottom of the mixing bowl. If the dough is still sticking to the sides of the bowl, turn the mixer on low and gently add an additional ¼ cup (30 g) of flour to the bowl and continue to mix.

Turn out the dough onto a clean surface that has been lightly floured. Knead the dough with your hands, pressing away from you, and then pulling the top of the dough back toward you to fold it over the bottom edge of dough. Rotate the dough 90 degrees, and repeat. Do this about 5 or 6 times until a smooth dough starts to form. Place the dough into a lightly greased bowl, and cover with plastic wrap. Let the dough rise in a warm place for about 60 to 90 minutes.

Once the dough has risen, turn it out onto a lightly floured surface, and divide it into 12 to 16 equal portions. Take each ball of dough and flatten it out into a disk. Add approximately 1 teaspoon (5 ml) of pesto and 1 cube of mozzarella to the middle of the disk. Fold all the edges together and crimp them tightly. Place the roll crimped-side down in the greased cast-iron skillet. Repeat with the remaining rolls. Be sure the rolls have enough room to grow a little more. You may need to bake them in batches, or you can freeze the extras on a parchment-lined baking sheet immediately after forming them. Once frozen, they can be moved to a freezer-safe plastic bag until you're ready to make them.

Brush the rolls with additional pesto if you have some, and then sprinkle with Parmesan cheese. Cover the rolls with plastic wrap and let them rise one more time for approximately 30 minutes. Preheat your oven to 350°F (176°C). Place the rolls into the oven and bake for 25 to 30 minutes or until golden brown on top and the cheese on top has melted. Serve them immediately; just watch your tongue!

Mixed-Berry-and-Mascarpone-Stuffed French Toast

Sweetened mascarpone mixed with fresh summer berries pair beautifully when stuffed inside fresh challah bread. Crispy on the outside and still warm and gooey on the inside, this is the perfect summer brunch dish or Mother's Day breakfast in bed.

SERVES: 5

1 loaf brioche, sliced 1½–2 in (4–5 cm) thick

1 cup (145 g) mixed berries, sliced if needed

4 oz (115 g) mascarpone cheese, softened

2 tbsp (25 g) sugar

2 tsp (10 ml) vanilla, divided

½ cup (120 ml) milk

3 eggs

½ tsp cinnamon

½ cup (75 g) pecans, chopped

Maple or berry syrup, for serving

Slice a small horizontal pocket into the middle of each slice of brioche using a sharp-pointed serrated knife. Make sure you don't puncture through the bread. Set aside.

In a bowl, mix together the berries, softened mascarpone, sugar and 1 teaspoon (5 ml) of the vanilla extract until smooth. With a spoon or knife, spread this mixture into the pocket of each bread slice.

In a shallow bowl, whisk together the milk, eggs, cinnamon and the remaining vanilla. Dip each slice of stuffed brioche into the egg wash and place into a heated nonstick-sprayed pan over medium to medium-high heat. Cook until each side is a deep golden brown, about 3 to 4 minutes per side. Serve immediately with additional berries or chopped pecans on top. Top with syrup for serving.

Meatless Monday and Beyond

When I married a farm boy, I had to learn to love vegetables. It wasn't that I *hated* them, but they were never a central part of every meal; they just existed on the plate, and I had no thought other than to eat them and get it over with. In the years since we have been together, the poking and prodding to have two different vegetables at dinner and finally taking chances cooking vegetables in ways I hadn't before finally got me on the plant-lover's bandwagon.

Eggs will always be a central part of my vegetarian focus, and they taste good on top of just about anything savory. But I have found many of these recipes have worked their way into our regular lunch and dinner rotation, even making wonderful leftovers for breakfasts, lunches and dinners on the go.

The Quiche Lorraine with Spinach in a Hash Brown Crust (page 143) is equally at home on a brunch buffet as it is at a breakfast-for-dinner night in. The Feta and Heirloom Tomato Bruschetta (page 140) is a crowd-pleaser that has been in my family for years and will disappear in the blink of an eye.

So while I may not have grown up a veggie-phile, I am firmly in Camp Veggie now.

Delicata Squash with Spinach and Eggs

A few years ago, I came to rely heavily on squash when I burned out on potatoes. At one point I couldn't even look a potato in the eye anymore. Get it? Eye? I crack myself up. Anyway, delicata squash became my go-to for its easy preparation (you don't have to peel it!) and similarity in texture to a potato when it is roasted or fried in a pan. I took one of my favorite breakfasts made with sweet potatoes and replaced it with delicata squash, and it has become my favorite way to start the day.

SERVES: 4

1 large delicata squash, seeded and cubed into ½-inch (1-cm) cubes

2 tbsp (30 ml) light olive oil

Salt and pepper

1 tsp (5 g) ground cumin or chili powder

¼ tsp red pepper flakes

12 oz (340 g) fresh spinach

4 eggs

In your skillet over medium heat, add the squash and drizzle it with the olive oil. Using a spatula, stir the squash to make sure it is evenly coated with olive oil. Sprinkle the squash with salt, pepper, cumin (or chili powder) and red pepper flakes. Add more or less pepper flakes depending on how spicy you want your squash. Sauté until the squash is fork-tender and golden brown on all sides, about 10 minutes. Set the squash aside on a plate.

Reduce the heat to medium-low. In the same pan, wilt the spinach in batches. Set it aside with the squash. Lastly, fry your eggs until the whites are set but the yolks are still runny, about 2 to 3 minutes per side. Divide the squash and spinach among 4 plates and serve with an egg on top.

NOTE: You can also roast your squash in your skillet if you don't want to fry it. Prepare the squash with olive oil and seasonings, and bake at 350°F (176°C) until fork-tender, about 20 minutes.

Herb and Goat Cheese Frittata

A frittata is just a fancy-sounding omelet that hasn't been flipped. There, I said it. But it is everything an omelet-flipping novice (like yours truly) can totally get behind. Frittatas look impressive, and they sound fancy, but no one needs to know that these single-dish darlings are such a cinch to make. Take the credit. You've earned it. Mix and match your favorite fresh herbs and cheeses for this beauty. If you're craving some added meat protein, cook it first and just add it!

SERVES: 4 to 6

½ cup (110 g) wilted spinach

8 eggs, lightly beaten

¼ cup (60 ml) half-and-half

½ cup (40 g) shredded Parmesan

2 tbsp (6 g) chopped chives

2 tbsp (11 g) chopped basil

¾ cup (204 g) goat cheese or whole-milk ricotta, divided

2 tbsp (30 ml) olive oil

1 large shallot (about ½ cup [78 g]), minced

2 cloves garlic, minced

Preheat your oven to 425°F (220°C).

If you are using fresh spinach, wilt it first in the skillet over medium-low heat, flipping it frequently with tongs until soft. Set it aside and when cool enough to handle, squeeze it to remove any excess moisture. Next, in your mixing bowl, lightly beat the eggs and half-and-half. Whisk in the spinach, Parmesan, chives, basil, other herbs of your choice and ½ cup (60 g) of the crumbled goat cheese. Set aside.

With your skillet on the stove over medium-low heat, add the olive oil and shallot, caramelizing them until they are nearly translucent and golden brown on the edges, about 2 to 3 minutes. Add the garlic and stir until it becomes fragrant, about 1 minute.

Pour the egg mixture into the hot skillet. Shake the pan vigorously to make sure the egg does not stick to the bottom, about 30 seconds. Gently dollop spoonfuls of the remaining goat cheese into the egg mixture using the handle of the spoon to gently streak the frittata with cheese. Once the mixture is about halfway set, place it in the oven to bake for 10 to 12 minutes, checking on it frequently to make sure the top is turning golden brown and not burning.

Remove it from the oven, and let it set for a few minutes before slicing to serve.

Dutch Oven Salad Niçoise

This isn't your usual boring leafy salad. This is a hearty, filling salad with so many flavors and textures that it will be your new favorite for summer dining. If you're into meal prepping for a busy week ahead while still eating healthfully, this salad is a great desk-side meal.

SERVES: 6

— o —

1 lb (452 g) baby potatoes, halved or quartered to equal sizes

1 lb (453 g) fresh green beans, trimmed and halved

½ tsp salt

½ tsp ground black pepper

2 tbsp (15 g) minced basil

2 tbsp (30 ml) lemon juice

2 tbsp (30 ml) olive oil

¼ cup (40 g) thinly sliced shallots

2 cups (500 g) cherry tomatoes, halved

6 hard-boiled eggs, sliced

½ cup (71 g) Niçoise olives, halved

Fill your Dutch oven halfway with water and salt heavily. Bring the water to a heavy simmer, add the potatoes and simmer for 5 minutes. Add the fresh green beans and simmer for another 5 minutes. Using a fork, test the doneness. The potatoes should resist the fork just a little bit. Right before draining the potatoes and beans, fill a mixing bowl with lots of ice and water. Drain the water from the potatoes and green beans, and then pour them into the ice bath to stop the cooking process.

When the potatoes and green beans are cooled, drain the ice bath water and get rid of any ice that remains. Add salt, pepper, basil, lemon juice and olive oil to the beans and potatoes. Toss to combine. Add the shallots and tomatoes, combining once more. Serve immediately or chilled. Just before serving, top with the hard-boiled eggs and Niçoise olives.

NOTE: If Niçoise olives are not available, use pitted kalamata olives.

Feta and Heirloom Tomato Bruschetta

My mom has been making this recipe for years, and it is always the first dish to be eaten up when it is laid out at any of her summer dinners or gatherings. What makes this dish extra special isn't only that it usually contains tomatoes from her own garden, but also that she toasts the bread in butter and garlic beforehand, making it extra crispy. The crisp, buttery bread is a delightful contrast to the fresh summer-warmed tomatoes. Simple is always best. But that doesn't mean simple can't be elevated.

SERVES: 4

1 lb (454 g) fresh heirloom tomatoes

6–8 fresh basil leaves

1 cup (240 g) crumbled feta

Salt and pepper

1 bakery baguette

2 tbsp (30 ml) canola or vegetable oil

2 tbsp (28 g) butter, divided

3 large garlic cloves, minced

Balsamic vinegar for topping (optional)

Dice your tomatoes into small chunks, placing them into a mixing bowl. Mince your basil leaves with a very sharp knife, and place them into the bowl with the tomatoes. Then add in the crumbled feta, and salt and pepper to taste. Gently stir the mixture together. Place the bowl into the fridge to chill while you work on the garlic toast.

Cut your baguette on a diagonal bias into ½-inch (1.5-cm) slices. Set them aside and preheat your pan with 1 tablespoon (15 ml) of oil and 1 tablespoon (14 g) of butter. When the oil and butter are simmering, gently run each slice of bread through the oil, flipping it over to coat the bread evenly on both sides. Leave the bread slices in the pan until they are golden brown on one side. Gently flip them over and continue to toast them until golden brown on the other side. When the bread is nearly done and golden brown, gently push it to the side and add half of the minced garlic to the pan. Run the toasted bread over the garlic and flip the bread so it is coated evenly with the garlic. Remove the bread and set it aside. Repeat this with the remaining oil, butter, bread and garlic, working in batches if necessary.

Next, top the warm bread with the cool feta bruschetta mix. Finally, drizzle with balsamic vinegar, if desired, and serve immediately.

> NOTE: Use a variety of tomatoes or different soft cheese crumbles to switch up your flavors. Try crumbled goat cheese if you're feeling daring!

Quiche Lorraine with Spinach in a Hash Brown Crust

Truth be told, pie crusts and I have never seen eye to eye. Instead, I opt for hash browns for my crust. The hash browns bake into a crunchy base that perfectly holds the creamy eggs inside of the quiche. If you opt to serve this cold, it's best to prepare the hash browns in the skillet according to the directions below, then bake the potatoes in a pie pan or tart dish instead of the skillet. You don't want to store cast iron in the fridge due to the moisture content. If you plan to serve this warm, preparing and baking the quiche in the skillet is grand. If you're pressed for time, use preshredded potatoes and prepare according to the package directions.

SERVES: 6 to 8

6 cups (1.5 kg) shredded potatoes

Salt and pepper

½ lb (225 g) bacon

1 tbsp (15 ml) vegetable oil

6 eggs

1 clove garlic, minced

½ cup (120 ml) heavy cream

¼ cup (60 ml) milk

3 tbsp (45 g) flour

½ tsp baking powder

½ tsp salt

¾ cup (100 g) frozen spinach, thawed and excess moisture removed

1 cup (108 g) shredded Gruyère cheese

NOTE: Change up your cheese selection with goat cheese or cheddar in lieu of Gruyère.

Preheat your oven to 350°F (176°C).

Place the potatoes in a large bowl filled with cold water. Let the potatoes sit for 10 minutes to remove excess starch that comes out when shredded. Drain and rinse potatoes until the water runs clean. You want to make sure you drain the potatoes well. Lay out several paper towels onto a clean surface. Pour the drained potatoes onto the paper towels and pat dry to remove excess moisture. Sprinkle with salt and pepper. If you are using preshredded potatoes, prepare them according to the package directions.

Prepare the bacon, frying until crispy.

In a large skillet, heat the oil until shimmering over medium-high heat. Pour the potatoes into the nonstick pan and press them into the bottom of the pan, forming a skillet-size potato pancake. Let the hash browns cook until they turn crispy and golden brown, about 10 minutes. Using two oven mitts and a large plate, very carefully invert the hash browns from the skillet onto the plate. Place the skillet back onto the burner, and then slide the uncooked side of the hash brown down from the plate into the skillet to cook until crispy and golden brown, another 10 minutes.

If you want to make this cold, slide the hash browns into a pie or tart pan. You will not want to store your skillet-baked quiche in the fridge.

In a large mixing bowl, whisk together the eggs, garlic, cream, milk, flour, baking powder and salt. Stir in the spinach and Gruyère cheese.

Pour the eggs and vegetables into the prepared hash brown crust right in the skillet, place it in the oven and bake until the center is set, about 45 minutes. Check after 35 minutes to ensure it does not overcook. Remove from oven and allow to cool slightly before serving.

Lemon Thyme and Mushroom Risotto

The best risottos are creamy, silky and delicious. Pairing that texture with fresh lemon, thyme and mushrooms make this an elegant one-pot meal for an elegant date night in or just a weeknight meal. Its ability to traverse any meal, family-style or elegant, makes this recipe a keeper.

SERVES: 4

3 tbsp (45 g) butter

8 oz (226 g) sliced cremini or other mushroom of your choice

1 large shallot, minced

2 cloves garlic, minced

1½ cups (300 g) arborio rice

⅔ cup (160 ml) white wine

5 cups (1 L) vegetable stock (or low-sodium chicken stock)

1 cup (90 g) grated Parmesan cheese

2 tsp (3 g) fresh minced thyme

1 tsp (5 g) lemon zest

Salt and pepper (optional)

Melt the butter in a skillet over medium heat. Add the sliced mushrooms and sauté until they soften and begin to turn golden brown, about 5 to 6 minutes. If the mushrooms are cooking too quickly, you can reduce the heat to medium-low. Add the shallot and sauté it with the mushrooms until they soften. Stir in the garlic as well until it becomes fragrant, about 1 minute. Pour in the arborio rice, and stir to combine it with the mushrooms.

Stirring constantly, pour in the white wine and allow it to nearly completely evaporate. Slowly continue to stir in the stock 1 cup (240 ml) at a time, making sure it nearly absorbs before adding another cup. If you reduced the heat to medium-low and the pan is not simmering, return the heat to medium. Stir the risotto constantly so the natural starch in the rice releases and it starts to look creamy.

When all the stock is added and the rice is nearly done, about 35 to 40 minutes, stir in the Parmesan cheese and sprinkle with fresh thyme and lemon zest. Add salt and pepper to taste if needed. Plate and serve!

Skillet-Roasted Tomatillo Salsa

This recipe is perfectly paired with the Peppered Pork Tenderloin Medallions (page 25). The beauty of this recipe combined with the pepper-crusted pork recipe is that it really is a one-skillet meal! Make this salsa for dipping or leave it chunky for topping on your favorite summer grilled meats like pork or chicken.

SERVES: 6

¾ lb (340 g) tomatillos, peeled, washed and quartered

¼ lb (115 g) white onion, chopped

5 garlic cloves, peeled

½–1 jalapeño, sliced, with or without seeds depending on taste (and level of desired heat)

3 tbsp (45 ml) vegetable oil

Salt and pepper to taste

1 lime, juiced

Place the tomatillos, white onion, garlic cloves and jalapeño into a 10-inch (25-cm) skillet and toss with vegetable oil. Season liberally with salt and pepper. Place the skillet on the stove at medium-high heat, and scorch the tomatillos until they are brown on all sides and the onions are charred and softening around the edges. This should take about 7 to 9 minutes. Remove the skillet from the heat, and let rest about 5 minutes.

Either use an immersion blender and puree the salsa right in the pan, or pour it into a blender or food processor and puree until a few chunks remain. Add the lime juice to taste. Chill the salsa and allow the flavors to meld, or serve immediately.

Cauliflower and Cashew Stir-Fry with Harissa

Root vegetables don't get the love they deserve. This casserole puts them center stage and pairs them with browned pork sausage and sourdough croutons on top for some added crunch. If you are looking for a side dish for your Thanksgiving dinner, this one will be requested again and again. I make this recipe both ways, vegetarian and with sausage, so choose which option works best for your diet and cravings.

SERVES: 4 to 6

1 large head cauliflower, cut into bite-size florets

3 tbsp (45 ml) extra-light olive oil

Salt and pepper to taste

1 bell pepper

1 cup (111 g) roasted cashews

2 tbsp (16 g) grated fresh ginger

6 oz (160 g) fresh snow peas

2 green onions, chopped

½ cup (120 ml) harissa sauce

2–3 tbsp (30–45 ml) soy sauce

Cilantro, for garnish

Preheat your oven to 450°F (230°C).

Place the cauliflower florets into a skillet and toss with olive oil. Sprinkle with salt and pepper. Roast the cauliflower for 10 to 12 minutes, tossing after 5 minutes to make sure the cauliflower is roasting on all sides.

While the cauliflower is roasting, seed and dice the bell pepper.

When the cauliflower is done roasting, it should be nearly fork-tender and slightly browned on the outside. Place the skillet on a large burner, and turn the heat on to medium. Stir in the cashews, grated ginger, snow peas, bell pepper and green onions. Cook until simmering and the bell peppers have just started to soften, about 3 to 4 minutes. Stir in harissa and soy sauces to taste, and garnish with cilantro just prior to serving.

Roasted Vegetable and Ricotta Polenta

Put your garden's bumper crop to work with this roasted vegetable polenta. Roast your favorite vegetables together to create a flavorful dish to serve to a crowd. Mix and match whatever vegetables you have on hand for this dish. You can roast, stir and serve all from one enameled casserole pan. Minimal cleanup means more time spending with friends or family, the way it should be. The creamy, cheesy polenta and crispy roasted vegetables go hand in hand for a comforting one-pot meal.

SERVES: 6

¼ cup (60 ml) olive oil, divided

1 sweet onion, chopped

2 Hatch or Anaheim chili peppers, seeded and diced

1 red bell pepper, seeded and diced

1 cup (2 oz [66 g]) mushrooms, sliced

2 medium zucchinis, diced

2 cloves garlic, minced

Salt and pepper

3½ cups (820 ml) chicken stock

1 cup (160 g) cornmeal

1 cup (250 g) whole-fat ricotta cheese

2 eggs

2 cups (240 g) shredded pepper jack or cheddar cheese

Preheat your oven to 425°F (220°C).

In a pan, toss half of the olive oil with all of the vegetables and the garlic, ensuring they are coated evenly. Sprinkle liberally with salt and pepper. Place the pan in the oven and roast for 15 to 20 minutes, until the vegetables soften and brown slightly. Stir the vegetables halfway through the roasting. Remove and set them aside on a plate.

Heat the pan on the stove over medium-low heat. Add the chicken stock and remaining olive oil. Slowly whisk in the cornmeal so it does not clump. Once it is stirred in, whisk in the ricotta, eggs and shredded cheese. The mixture should be bubbling prior to tasting to avoid eating raw egg. Taste the mixture to ensure it is seasoned to your liking, adding more salt and pepper if needed. Top the polenta with the roasted vegetables, and bake for 10 minutes to set the polenta. Serve right out of the pan.

Tomato Tart with Whipped Ricotta

Tomatoes fresh from the garden are the highlight of summer, and this dish is a perfect complement to a warm night and a glass of chilled white wine. Flaky puff pastry and whipped herbed ricotta are a great pair with thinly sliced heirloom tomatoes. Mix and match dried or fresh herbs that you have on hand to customize this tart!

SERVES: 24

2 sheets puff pastry, thawed

¾–1 cup (180–240 g) heirloom tomatoes of various sizes and types

1 cup (250 g) ricotta cheese

2 eggs, divided

1½ tsp (5 g) salt

1 tbsp (2 g) dried mixed herbs of your choice

2 tbsp (15 g) minced shallots

Preheat your oven to 400°F (205°C).

On a cleaned and floured surface, roll out the puff pastry sheets into 10 × 10 inch (25 × 25 cm) squares. Using your pizza cutter, cut the corners off the puff pastry to create a circle. With the excess puff pastry, cut out small shapes with cookie cutters.

Slice the tomatoes as thinly as possible, and then place them in between paper towels to wick away any remaining moisture. While these are resting, turn to the ricotta.

In a small bowl, whip the ricotta with 1 egg, salt, mixed herbs and the shallots. Spread half of the ricotta onto the middle of the puff pastry sheet to within ¾ inch (2 cm) of the puff pastry edge. Set aside the other half of the ricotta for the next tart. Top the ricotta with half of the thinly sliced heirloom tomatoes. Place it into the skillet. Prepare the egg wash by mixing together 1 egg and 1 tablespoon (15 ml) of water. Brush the edge of the puff pastry with the egg wash. If you've cut out any decorative pieces of puff pastry, also brush those with the egg wash and place them on top of the tomatoes in the skillet. Bake for 25 to 30 minutes or until the edges are golden brown. Remove the tart from the skillet and slice with the pizza cutter. Serve immediately. Repeat with the other puff pastry for more servings because this will go fast!

For Your Sweet Tooth

When we were kids, my brother would say that his "dinner tummy" was full, but his "dessert tummy" was always ready. That about sums up my feelings now, as an adult. No matter how full I am after a good dinner, I will always find room for dessert. Always.

When I was a kid, my stepdad wowed us with Cherries Jubilee set ablaze (page 158), and I fell head over heels in love with chocolate hazelnut spread, thanks to my grandma. The Triple Chocolate and Nutella Skillet Brownie (page 161) and Nutella-and-Fudge-Stuffed Skillet Cookie (page 170) are testaments to my undying love of the stuff.

For nights that you are craving something a little more highbrow, go for the Bananas Foster for One (or More) (page 165) or the Roasted Pears with Chardonnay Caramel Sauce (page 169). Everything in this book is cooked with your dish count in mind so that you can enjoy dessert without a mountain of dishes behind you to wash away all your good cheer.

Let's see what inspires you today!

Blueberry, Cardamom and Coconut Crumble

It's okay when you don't want to share. This dish can be made in a large skillet for a crowd or in smaller skillets if you are practicing portion control. But a little sin in a skillet is good for the soul. This crumble shouts SUMMER, with fresh blueberries and shredded coconut. But it also fits perfectly into fall with spicy, warm cardamom.

SERVINGS: 4

4 heaping cups (592 g) blueberries (fresh or frozen)

½ cup (38 g) shredded coconut

½ cup (100 g) sugar

2 tbsp (15 g) corn starch (plus 1 tsp [8 g], as needed, with frozen blueberries to soak up extra juices)

1 tbsp (15 g) lemon zest

2 tbsp (30 ml) lemon juice

⅔ cup (80 g) flour

⅔ cup (120 g) brown sugar

⅔ cup (60 g) oats

¼–½ tsp ground cardamom

¼ tsp salt

6–8 tbsp (90–120 g) butter, cubed

Ice cream (optional)

Preheat your oven to 350°F (176°C).

In your cast-iron skillet, add the blueberries. Sprinkle the blueberries with coconut, sugar and corn starch. Toss to coat the blueberries completely. Next, sprinkle the blueberries with lemon zest and lemon juice. Toss to combine again. A sugar sauce will start to form at this stage.

In a mixing bowl, whisk together the flour, brown sugar, oats, cardamom and salt. Add 6 tablespoons (90 g) of butter to the flour and oat mixture, and blend it with a pastry blender or your hands. Blend the oat mixture until large crumbles form, about 2 to 3 minutes. If the mixture looks dry, add the remaining butter and blend together. Sprinkle the crumble over the mixed blueberries and bake for 30 to 40 minutes. If you choose to bake these in individual dishes, reduce your baking time to 25 to 30 minutes, checking after 20 minutes just to ensure the crumble is not burning.

Be sure you top with your favorite ice cream before serving!

NOTE: If you can't find cardamom, substitute with ground ginger.

Cherries Jubilee

The first time that my stepdad ever made this was when I was about eight years old. I was captivated that he set something on fire and it did not burn the house down, and that it tasted so gosh-darn good. It always struck me as a special occasion dessert, but having made it myself (repeatedly), I find it is every bit an everyday dessert as well. The ingredients are simple, the presentation is equally rustic as it is elegant, and, well, when you set things on fire, everyone will be impressed.

SERVES: 4

1 lb (453 g) frozen or fresh sweet cherries, pitted

2 tbsp (30 g) unsalted butter

½ cup (95 g) brown sugar

½ tsp orange zest (optional)

¼ cup (60 ml) brandy

1 pt (288 g) vanilla ice cream or gelato

Place the cherries into a skillet over medium heat and stir to release the juice and soften slightly, about 3 minutes. Add the butter, and whisk in the brown sugar to form a light caramel sauce. Bring the mixture to a simmer until the sugar dissolves and thickens slightly, about 5 minutes. Add orange zest if desired.

Remove the skillet from the heat, and slowly pour in the brandy, or whatever alcohol is being used. Return the pan to the stove and turn it on to medium-low heat until the pan ignites, or use a long match or lighter to ignite, and allow the brandy to burn off.

Immediately spoon over vanilla ice cream and serve. If serving in small skillets for individuals, just add the ice cream into the skillet and serve.

NOTE: Use other alcohols, like rum or bourbon, to give this dessert a different flavor.

Triple Chocolate and Nutella Skillet Brownie

If you have been around my blog for any length of time, you know that this recipe is my pride and joy for many reasons, not least of which is that it has three types of chocolate, one being nearly a whole cup of Nutella. My grandmother instilled in me a deep love of the stuff from an early age, and it continues growing in magnitude to this day. Plus, everyone loves a piping-hot brownie in a skillet.

SERVES: 8 to 10

½ cup (120 g) butter, melted and cooled

¾ cup (220 g) Nutella or chocolate hazelnut spread

½ cup (100 g) brown sugar or coconut sugar

½ cup (100 g) white sugar

2 eggs

1 tsp (5 ml) vanilla

1⅔ cups (200 g) flour

½ tsp salt

1 tsp (5 g) baking soda

2 tbsp (14 g) cocoa powder

1 cup (170 g) semisweet chocolate chips, divided

½ cup (80 g) toffee pieces, divided

Ice cream (optional)

Preheat your oven to 350°F (176°C).

In a large bowl, whisk or use a spatula to combine butter, chocolate hazelnut spread (like Nutella), brown and white sugar, eggs and vanilla until smooth. In another mixing bowl, whisk together the flour, salt, baking soda and cocoa powder until fluffy. Using a spatula, gently fold the flour mixture into the butter-and-egg mixture until there are only one or two small streaks of flour that remain.

Fold three quarters of the chocolate chips and ¼ cup (40 g) of the toffee pieces into the mix. Fold only until the chips and toffee are incorporated into the mix.

Spoon the batter into a cast-iron skillet that has been sprayed with a nonstick spray. Even the batter out and press to within ½ inch (1.5 cm) of the edge of the skillet—the brownie will spread out—to leave room between the batter and the side of the skillet so the edges don't overcook.

Top with the remaining chocolate chips and toffee bits. Place in the oven and bake for 20 to 25 minutes or until the edges are set and a toothpick placed in the middle of the brownie comes out clean.

Let the brownie cool on a wire rack in the skillet until just warm, about 45 minutes. This will be the longest 45 minutes of your life. It will still be very soft in the middle, but as it cools, the brownie will set entirely.

Drizzle with additional softened Nutella if desired or top with ice cream!

NOTE: You can make this skillet brownie entirely in the skillet to reduce your dish count, or use two mixing bowls and just bake it in your skillet. It's totally up to you.

Apricot-Orange Cornmeal Cake

Lighter, fluffier and sweeter than traditional corn bread, this is more like a cross between coffee cake and corn bread. Add some orange juice and zest for an extra punch and sprinkle with apricots to make this summer surprise. We kept coming back to this dessert again and again, sneaking little slices because it was so irresistible. If you want to make this for the holidays, macerate some cranberries and substitute them for the apricots!

SERVES: 10

½ cup (120 ml) light olive oil

2 eggs

1 cup + ¼ cup (250 g)

½ cup (120 ml) orange juice

1 orange, zested

1½ cups (180 g) all-purpose flour

½ cup (70 g) finely ground yellow cornmeal

2 tsp (8 g) baking powder

½ tsp salt

1 cup (151 g) fresh chopped apricots

Preheat your oven to 375°F (190°C).

In your skillet, whisk together the olive oil, eggs and 1 cup (200 g) of sugar until light and fluffy. Slowly whisk in the orange juice and orange zest. Next, sprinkle the flour, cornmeal, baking powder and salt over the top. Since you are not mixing the dry ingredients beforehand as you normally would, ensure the dry ingredients are thoroughly distributed over the top of the wet mixture. Gently fold the dry ingredients into the wet ingredients until only a few steaks of flour remain. Fold in the apricots until they are just combined. Do not overmix. Spread the batter evenly into the skillet and sprinkle the remaining ¼ cup (50 g) of sugar over the top. Bake for 20 to 25 minutes or until a toothpick inserted into the pan comes out clean. Cool in the skillet for about 20 minutes, then remove it from the pan and allow it to complete cooling on a wire rack.

NOTE: If you're using a new and unseasoned cast iron pan, line it with parchment paper to ensure the cake doesn't stick during baking.

Bananas Foster for One (or More!)

This dessert, with caramelized bananas and a little dark rum for a tiny kick, is ultra-decadent. The added sea salt gives these bananas an extra luxurious dimension. The greener the bananas the better! Ripe bananas with spots will turn to mush if not handled carefully. You can easily multiply these ingredients to make more than one serving for you and a friend—or just double for you!

SERVINGS: 1 (or more)

2 tbsp (30 g) butter

¼ cup (50 g) brown sugar

¼ tsp ground cinnamon

1 heavy pinch of nutmeg

1 banana, cut in half, and then sliced lengthwise

2 tbsp (30 ml) dark rum, such as Meyer's

1 scoop vanilla ice cream

Pinch of sea salt

Heat your skillet over medium to medium-high heat. In the skillet, whisk together the butter, brown sugar, cinnamon and nutmeg until the sugar starts to dissolve. Add the sliced bananas cut side down, and let them fry until they begin to brown, about 3 minutes. Gently flip each slice over and fry on the other side for another 2 to 3 minutes. Very gently pour the rum into the pan, and watch for the pan to catch fire! If it doesn't catch right away, use a stick lighter to ignite it. Let the fire burn down completely. Test the bananas with a fork to see if they have softened. Remove them from the heat. Top with ice cream and sprinkle with sea salt for an additional twist. Serve immediately.

NOTE: If you don't want to play with fire, omit the dark rum and use rum extract. Or omit the rum altogether; caramelized bananas are delightful on their own!

Double-Chocolate Fudge Skillet Poke Cake

Dark chocolate hot fudge is poured over a fluffy, cocoa skillet cake, finding its way into every nook and cranny for a double dose of chocolate in every bite—with homemade whipped cream on top, naturally. Now, I'm the first to admit that poke cakes aren't typically on the spectrum of elegant desserts, but when they are made with high-quality ingredients and from scratch, they can solidify their status among their elegant dessert counterparts. And this cake is no exception.

SERVES: 8

1 cup (200 g) white sugar

1 scant cup (120 g) all-purpose flour

⅔ cup (65 g) unsweetened cocoa powder

¾ tsp baking powder

¾ tsp baking soda

½ tsp salt

1 whole egg

½ cup (120 ml) milk

¼ cup (60 ml) vegetable oil

1 tsp (5 ml) vanilla extract

⅓ cup (80 ml) boiling water

1 cup (240 ml) heavy whipping cream

2 tbsp (25 g) sugar

½ tsp vanilla extract

½ cup (120 ml) high-quality hot fudge, warmed

Preheat your oven to 350°F (176°C).

In a large bowl, stir together the sugar, flour, cocoa, baking powder, baking soda and salt. Add the egg, milk, oil and vanilla, and mix together until smooth. Slowly whisk in the boiling water to temper the eggs and not curdle them. The batter will be thin, but this is normal. Pour the batter into a greased skillet and bake for 30 minutes or until a toothpick inserted into the center comes out clean. Immediately place the skillet on a wire rack to cool.

While the cake cools, whip together the whipping cream, sugar and vanilla in a clean mixing bowl until stiff peaks form, about 5 to 7 minutes. Refrigerate until ready to use.

When the cake is cooled, use a chop stick or the back of a wooden spoon to poke holes directly into the cake to create miniature wells. Spoon the hot fudge over the cake, filling the holes. Top with the whipped cream, spread it over the cake and serve.

NOTE: Switch up the fudge sauce for a high-quality salted caramel!

Roasted Pears with Chardonnay Caramel Sauce

One of my favorite fruits all year long is the humble pear. It is beautiful and so versatile to cook or bake with. These roasted pears create much of their own syrupy sauce when roasting; you do only a little work to make this dish truly special. If you don't have a chardonnay in mind, use apple cider instead, making this family friendly in the process.

SERVES: 6

4 tbsp (60 g) unsalted butter

¼ cup (47 g) brown sugar

½ tsp ground cinnamon

1 tsp (2 g) freshly grated ginger

3 Bartlett pears, cut in half from stem to base, seeds removed

¼ cup (60 ml) chardonnay

⅓ cup (80 ml) apple cider

1½ tsp (5 g) cornstarch

½ cup (75 g) toasted chopped pecans

Pinch of salt

Heavy cream (optional)

Preheat your oven to 450°F (230°C).

Melt your butter and brown sugar together in a skillet over medium heat, stirring until the sugar is dissolved. Whisk in the cinnamon and ginger. Add the pears cut-side down and fry for 3 to 4 minutes until they begin to turn golden brown. Gently turn them over onto the round outer side, and pour in the wine to briefly deglaze the pan. Place the skillet into the oven and roast the pears for about 10 minutes until they are soft.

Once the pears are done, gently remove them from the skillet, and put them on a plate. With the remaining juices in the pan, whisk in the apple cider and cornstarch to thicken the sauce. Start with 1 teaspoon (3 g) of cornstarch and add in the remainder if needed. Bring the mixture to a simmer on the stove, whisking constantly until thickened, about 2 to 4 minutes. Stir in the toasted pecans and toss them in the sauce to combine. Add a pinch of salt to cut the sweetness if it's not to your liking. It will create an added dimension to the dish. Pour the sauce over the pears and serve immediately. Drizzle with heavy cream on top if desired.

Nutella-and-Fudge-Stuffed Skillet Cookie

The skillet cookie has hit the Pinterest generation hard, and I'm not immune to its charms, either. These cookies are everywhere and in so many forms that they're almost becoming inelegant! But it sealed the deal for me when Ben and I were on a vacation in Wyoming, and the hotel—a Four Seasons, no less—was serving them in their dining rooms. So, if skillet cookies can be served in five-star hotels, they are elevated enough for me. You can make this cookie in one skillet if you wish, or opt for the mixer version and just bake it in a skillet. Either way, it's a skillet-baking necessity.

SERVES: 8 to 10

1 cup (240 g) butter, cubed

1 cup (190 g) brown sugar

½ cup (100 g) white sugar

2 eggs

2½ tsp (12 ml) vanilla

2¼ cups (270 g) flour

¼ tsp salt

½ tsp baking soda

2 cups (340 g) semisweet chocolate chips

½ cup (150 g) chocolate hazelnut spread, like Nutella

Preheat your oven to 300°F (150°C).

In one mixing bowl, beat together the cubed butter, brown sugar and white sugar until light and fluffy. Beat in the eggs one at a time, scraping down the sides of the bowl between additions. Next, whisk in the vanilla extract.

In a second bowl, whisk together the flour, salt and baking soda. Mix the dry ingredients into the wet ingredients until just incorporated. Stir in the chocolate chips until just combined.

Press half of the cookie dough into a pan, leaving a ½-inch (1.5-cm) gap between the dough edge and the sides of the pan. Spread the Nutella out over the cookie dough within a ½ inch (1.5 cm) of the edges of the cookie dough. Press the other half of the cookie dough over the top, sealing the edges to contain the Nutella.

Bake for 22 to 25 minutes until the dough is just set and the middle of the cookie looks slightly underdone. The residual heat from the pan will continue to bake the cookie slightly. Allow the pan to cool on a wire rack until it's ready to serve.

NOTE: If chocolate hazelnut spread isn't your thing, fill this cookie with fudge or caramel, or omit it entirely and just go straight cookie!

Cookie Butter Swirl S'mores Dip

Let's not pretend that we don't all want to dive headfirst into a skillet of melted and swirled speculoos, or cookie butter, and chocolate chip action. That is, once we get past the top layer of toasted marshmallow cream. Sometimes "elevated" dishes need to take a back seat to the fun and simple. The best part is that this sweet dip doesn't require a campfire.

SERVES: 6

⅔ cup (222 g) speculoos, or cookie butter, such as Biscoff

1 cup (170 g) semisweet chocolate chips

1 cup (128 g) marshmallow creme

Graham crackers, for dipping

Preheat your oven to 375°F (190°C).

Spread the cookie butter over the bottom of a skillet. Sprinkle with chocolate chips, and dollop marshmallow creme on top. The creme will settle and spread, so it will not need to look perfect.

Place the skillet in the oven, for 10 to 15 minutes, until the marshmallow on top is toasted and golden brown. Remove the skillet from the oven and let stand for 5 minutes before serving. Serve with graham crackers or other cookies.

NOTE: Substitute the cookie butter with peanut butter or other flavored nut butter for a seasonal change.

Half-Assed Apple Pie

I'm not pie proficient by any means. All my crusts come out oddly shaped and lopsided, and that's if they don't fall apart in the process of getting them into the pie plate. But I do love pie, and this Half-Assed Apple Pie fills my pie cravings, and I don't have to get flummoxed by my inability to roll out a pretty crust. There are a few cheats to make this pie easy, and you don't have to wait hours for it to cook and cool. Sautéing the apples in butter and caramelizing them in sugar speeds up the process and keeps all those cozy flavors you love without spending time waiting around for a pie to cool. When pie is at stake, it is not the time to practice patience. Add caramel sauce, cranberries or pecans to the apple mixture for seasonal changes.

SERVES: 6

6 large apples, Honeycrisp, Braeburn, Granny Smith or a mix of others

8 tbsp (120 g) butter, cubed

1 cup (200 g) sugar

2 tbsp (12 g) apple pie spice

¼ cup (30 g) all-purpose flour

1 prepared, packaged 9" pie crust

1 egg

1 tbsp (15 ml) water

1 pt (288 g) ice cream

Preheat your oven to 425°F (220°C).

Cut the apples into quarter-size chunks and set aside in a large mixing bowl.

In your skillet over medium-high heat, add the cubed butter and melt it. When the butter starts to simmer, add the chunked apples. Sauté your apples, turning them over every 2 minutes or so until they are about halfway cooked through, about 6 minutes. While they are cooking, sprinkle the apples with the sugar, apple pie spice and flour. Mix the apples and spices together, continuing to cook the apples. The mixture should thicken. This process will take about 15 minutes total.

While the apples are doing their business, roll out the pie crust, crimp the edges and cut three holes on top, or use small cookie cutters to cut out decorative shapes to top your apple pie.

Place the pie crust over the top of the half-cooked apples. If you are using cutouts, arrange them over the top. Brush the pie crust with a mixture of egg and water. Bake the pie for 30 minutes or until the top crust is golden brown. Remove the pie from the oven and allow it to cool on a wire rack for at least 30 minutes before serving. And, naturally, top with ice cream before serving!

NOTE: Cut out shapes with cookie cutters to create a fun design on the top crust.

Maple and Butternut Squash Custard

Family-style desserts like my favorite Blueberry, Cardamom and Coconut Crumble (page 157) and the famed Triple Chocolate and Nutella Skillet Brownie (page 161) bring people together. These will always have a place at the center of my table, and hopefully yours, too. Another family-style dessert, this custard is reminiscent of your favorite Thanksgiving pie—pumpkin pie—but without the dreaded pie crust sculpting. The filling is always the best part anyway.

SERVES: 6 to 8

3 eggs

1 (15-oz [425-g]) can butternut squash puree

1½ cups (360 ml) whipping cream

½ cup + ¼ cup (143 g) brown sugar, divided

¼ cup (60 ml) pure maple syrup

1 tsp (5 g) pumpkin pie spice

Pinch of salt

¼ cup (30 g) flour

¼ cup (56 g) butter, softened

¼ cup (28 g) chopped pecans

Preheat your oven to 350°F (176°C).

In a well-seasoned skillet, whisk together the eggs, squash puree, whipping cream, brown sugar, maple syrup, pumpkin pie spice and salt one at a time, ensuring the mixture is smooth in between additions. Scrape down the sides of the skillet as you go to make sure it is all mixing thoroughly. Bake the custard in the skillet for 25 minutes.

While the custard is baking, make the crumble in a mixing bowl by blending together the flour, sugar, butter and pecans with your fingers. The crumble should resemble coarse sand with pecans. Place the mixture in the fridge until the initial 25-minute baking is up. Sprinkle the crumble artistically over the top of the custard and bake for another 15 minutes or until a knife inserted into the middle comes out clean.

Remove it from the oven, and place it on a wire rack to cool. Serve warm about an hour after baking.

NOTE: You can often find butternut squash puree right next to the pumpkin puree at your store. If it is not available, just use pumpkin or sweet potato.

Sweet Potato Bake with Coconut-Pecan Crumble

This is a family favorite of Ben's, requested every Thanksgiving. It's equal parts dessert and side dish, but serve it along with some ice cream and you've got it made. Whip everything together in one pan, using a food processor or masher only to break apart your sweet potatoes. It's easy as pie. Easier in fact!

SERVES: 8

4–5 sweet potatoes (4 lb [1.8 kg]), peeled and cubed

1 tsp (5 ml) vanilla

6 tbsp (90 g) butter, softened

½ cup (120 ml) milk

2 eggs, beaten

¾ cup (150 g) sugar

1 cup (76 g) coconut

1 cup (180 g) brown sugar

1 cup (121 g) pecans or walnuts, chopped

¾ cup (90 g) flour

6 tbsp (90 g) butter, melted

Preheat your oven to 375°F (190°C).

In your Dutch oven or braiser, bring water to a boil. Add the sweet potatoes and simmer just until the potatoes are fork-tender, about 15 minutes. Drain into a colander, and place them back into the Dutch oven. With a hand mixer, beat the potatoes until smooth, breaking apart as many large pieces as possible. Beat in the vanilla, softened butter, milk, beaten eggs and sugar. Beat everything together until the butter has melted and everything is evenly dispersed.

In a bowl, mix together the coconut, brown sugar, chopped pecans and flour. Stir in the melted butter and mix until it starts to look like pea-size crumbles. Sprinkle over the top of the sweet potatoes. Place it in the oven and bake uncovered for 20 to 25 minutes, or until the top is golden brown. Serve warm.

NOTE: This dish can be made a day or two ahead of time, and then baked the day of. You may need to increase the time of baking if it comes straight out of the fridge and into the oven. If you are going to make this and bake it later, prepare it in a baking dish that can go from the fridge to the oven safely.

ENAMELED CAST IRON

If a big, beautiful and shiny porcelain enameled pan has graced you with its presence, wash that, too. The beauty of enameled pans is that they are coated in nonreactive porcelain, and they don't require the seasoning that standard cast-iron pans do. That also means you can use soap!

Use a soft nonscuff sponge and dish soap to clean your pans. The porcelain may tarnish over time and with heavy cooking, but do not fear, your pans are not ruined. Keep on cooking.

Dry them thoroughly and they are ready for their next use.

TO SOAP OR NOT TO SOAP

In the world of cast-iron cooking, using soap can be a controversial topic. It is even controversial within my own family! You should see our holiday dinners. We get all heated up about this . . . kidding. But, when I found out my own mother was a soaper, it's like my world changed. Was up down? Was mac and cheese not the most perfect meal on the planet?

Okay, fine. That's all perhaps a little melodramatic, but it shocked me. Especially given the family story about what happened when my grandfather completely ruined the seasoning on my grandmother's pans, which she had spent years building up! One day, he took her pans to work and sandblasted them all, thinking he was doing her a favor. Little did he know that one of those newly sandblasted pans would come swinging his way. So when you hear talk about seasoned pans being gold in the kitchen, it's serious business.

Those same once-sandblasted pans still live on in our house to this day. They are a true family heirloom. And we still get a good laugh out of it 50 years later.

When my mother and I were cooking one day, and she started to wash her pans with soap, it stopped me dead in my tracks. I had to ask why she was soaping her pans. For her, these pans had been worn smooth from years of cooking, they were practically nonstick, and you could fry an egg in them! So whether it was from the years of use—these were the aforementioned grandmother's sandblasted pans—or the soaping, she knew what she liked and she did what she did.

For me, since my pans are still considered babies in the world of cast iron, I know that not soaping my pans is the best for me.

Whatever camp you pick, do what works best for you.

Next, it's time for the seasoning!

HOW TO SEASON YOUR CAST IRON

As we have established, the standard cast-iron pans are the ones that require seasoning. There are several ways you can do this. For starters, you need to know what kind of cooking you will be doing in your pan. For most everyday uses, I use canola oil as my seasoning agent. It has a higher smoke point than standard vegetable oil, making it better for pans that are frequently used for searing, and it doesn't leave a residual aftertaste or odor that some other oils or fats can.

Using butter can be problematic because of its low smoke point, approximately 350°F (176°C). Bacon is a good option; it has a moderate smoke point of about 370°F (185°C). And let's be honest. This means you get a pan full of hot bacon out of the deal. The only downside is that your pan will have a bacon tone to it that could release onto other foods. So it may not be the best option if you intend to cook sweet foods in that same cast iron.

Using everyday fats like these or vegetable shortening is just fine. But if you are intent on doing heavy searing, I recommend using something with a higher smoke threshold.

Vegetable oil is a great option that gets you into the 400°F (205°C) range. It is a good option since it is always available in my cupboard and is considered to be a neutral oil. It covers the range of heat most home cooks like us need on a regular basis.

For the heavy hitters, you can always turn to safflower oil, clarified butter or refined olive oil for super-high-heat-tolerant seasoning agents.

STOVETOP SEASONING

Now that you have picked your oil or seasoning agent of choice, place your newly washed and dried pan onto the stove and turn the burner up to medium heat. Medium heat will allow your pan to heat up completely, expand (as iron does) and typically not bring it to a smoking point. If your pan starts to smoke, turn the heat down slightly.

Next, grab a pair of cooking tongs and a few clean, wadded paper towels to dip or douse in a small amount of oil. Rub the paper towels around all of the interior surfaces of your heated-up cast-iron pan, even up the sides, creating a very thin layer of oil around the pan. Turn the heat off on the burner and let your pan cool down completely.

Once it is cool, do a double check to make sure that your pan does not have any pools of oil on the bottom. Only a very thin layer of oil is required, so mop up any residual oil if you can. Now you can use the pan or store it in a dry place.

This is my chosen method of seasoning pans. My skillets live on the top of my stove since they are my go-to pans, meaning seasoning is frequent and must be done quickly. At the end of a very long day of cooking, I will clean and reseason any pans I used that day so they are ready for my next bout of cooking.

OVEN SEASONING

If you're on a low and slow kick, you can also bake the seasoning onto your pans. Preheat your oven to 350°F (176°C). Clean your pans as you would normally do, with a bristled brush and some hot water, then dry them with paper towels. Next, place your pan into the oven for 15 minutes to complete the drying process. You don't want to add any oil to the pan if there is a chance some moisture may still be lingering. Oil will trap the water onto your cast iron and that runs the risk of creating rust—the kryptonite of cast iron.

Carefully remove your cast iron from the oven while it's hot, and use a wadded paper towel to smear a thin veil of oil around all the sides of the interior of your pan. Next, place it back in the oven for 30 minutes. After 30 minutes is up, turn off the heat and crack your oven to slowly cool down your pan. Once your pan is cool, remove it from the oven, check for any pooling of oil, wipe it away and store it for next time.

HEAVY-DUTY CLEANING

One key tool in your cleaning arsenal should be a pan scraper. It's a little plastic tool available at most kitchen or home goods stores. About the size of a credit card, it will help you scrape off the large hunks of cooked-on crisps that might be left after your culinary adventures.

Brush it real good. A sturdy-bristled brush is a must-have for caring for your cast iron. This will remove any layers of cooking oil or tidbits left behind.

If your pan has some serious gunk baked in, you can always fill the pan with ½ inch (1.5 cm) of water and bring the pan to a simmer on the stove at medium heat. This will help release any pieces too stubborn to come off on their own. Once that is done, continue to brush and scrape your pans as needed to remove left-behind crumbs.

Avoid using metal scouring pads on your cast iron unless you see rust setting in. These will quickly eat away at your hard-earned seasoning.

Another tried-and-true way to clean your cast iron is with course sea salt or kosher salt and a towel. Scrub the pan interior with salt while the pan is warm, and wipe away any gunk left behind. Once that is done, rinse your pan with hot water, and dry it completely on your stove over low heat, spraying lightly with a thin film of oil to keep moisture away. Bingo!

PEARLY WHITES—CLEANING ENAMELED CAST IRON

One of the beauties of enameled cast iron is that it doesn't require the seasoning that is typical for traditional cast iron. You can use soap, water and your favorite nonscouring sponge to clean it up. But there are always those odd instances where the white may have become discolored during the cooking process. The pan is not ruined, but it's just not pearly white like it was the day you brought it home from the store. Fear not! There are a couple of tricks I found that help keep my pans looking pretty and operating per usual.

Baking soda isn't just for baking. In this instance, my go-to is to make a paste of 1 part baking soda to 2 parts water. In a small bowl, whisk together your baking soda and water until a soft paste forms. Add more or less water depending on your needs. Using a wad of paper towels and a little elbow grease, rub your cleaned enameled pans with the mixture to remove any stains that might be present. This will help release some of those stubborn stains that just don't come away with traditional soap-and-water cleaning. The baking soda will take on a tan tint, so you'll know it's working.

You can also use products like Magic Erasers or nonscouring powders that are available on the market that can help clean your porcelain enameled pans. Just ensure that your pans have been cleaned completely prior to any cooking after using heavy-duty cleaning agents. And do not use these methods on your plain cast iron; they will harm your seasoning!

TO THE RESCUE

If, despite your best intentions and efforts, you see some rust setting in, what do you do? Many a pan has been rescued from such transgressions, and yours can be too!

Follow the seasoning guide above for stovetop or oven seasoning. Once the rust is gone, start getting your coating back with standard seasoning practices.

THE KEYS TO CAST IRON

- Moisture is bad. Don't allow any moisture to linger on your pans. This will risk rust setting in.

- You can use light soap or detergent if you wish on your pans. It won't kill them.

- Season with high-quality and high-smoke-point oils or fats.

- Seasoning gets better the more you cook with your pans.

- You can use metal utensils on plain cast-iron pans but not on enameled cast iron.

- Enameled cast iron's porcelain coating can chip; treat it like nonstick to keep it looking nice for a long time.

- Don't use harsh chemicals or scouring sponges on your cast iron.

COMMON OIL TYPE	SMOKE POINT	FLAVOR NEUTRAL	GOOD FOR
Butter	350°F (176°C)	No	Sautéing, Baking
Coconut Oil	350°F (176°C)	No	Sautéing, Baking, Roasting
Vegetable Oil/ Canola Oil	400°F (205°C)	Yes	Pan-frying, Deep-frying, Baking, Roasting
Extra-Virgin Olive Oil	375°F–400°F (190°C–205°C)	No	Sautéing, Pan-frying
Grapeseed Oil	400°F (205°C)	No	Sautéing, Roasting, Searing
Light Olive Oil	475°F (240°C)	Yes	Sautéing, Baking, Pan-frying
Clarified Butter	450°F (230°C)	No	Sautéing, Baking, Frying, Pan-frying, Roasting
Extra-Light Olive Oil	450°F (230°C)	No	Searing, Frying, Deep-frying
Safflower Oil	450°F (230°C)	Yes	Searing, Frying, Deep-frying

Acknowledgments

It goes without saying that my husband, Ben, and my trusty "labradork," Huck, need to be thanked for their love and emotional support for me while I was writing this book. They always encouraged me, one with hugs, the other with tail wags and sad seal eyes. I am so fortunate to spend my life's adventure with them.

To the rest of my family, thank you for being my cheering section, all instilling in me a part of yourselves and your love of food. If cooking is our love language, it's not a bad way to show our love.

Beka, Moonpie and Schmoopie: We have been through some serious cooking fiascos and adventures together. From the Great Chicken Incident to crunchy macaroni and cheese, and learning the art of the brisket—thank you for choking down the cooking disaster, and for being "my person" all these years.

My One Kitchen Many Hearts sisterhood: Kirsten, Jeanne, Mads, Kat and Allison. The brain trust is strong, and I am forever grateful for you all. You keep me together.

Sara and Corrine: My lifeline, alter egos, my sunshine. I love you.

Taryn and Jackie: What more could I ask for? My people.

Lauren, Julie, Gina, Brandy, Rachel, Rebecca, Laurie, Kita, Amanda and Meagan: You are marvels and my blogging safe space. What would I do without you, your encouragement and your ability to make me laugh on the daily?

Cathie Patt: Thank you for being part of my team and always checking my sanity while I wrote this book. It's not an easy feat, and you have helped me more than you know.

All the people I have worked with in my daily 9 to 5 and who have been force-fed leftovers and become taste testers extraordinaire. Thank you for suffering through it all with a smile. Particularly to the whole NorthSTAR Project team who have been overwhelmingly supportive of me while I was writing this book, thank you, guys, thank you, especially Kabri, April, Collette, Jim, Jeff and even you, Gabe. I love spending my days with people whose love of food rival my own and who can all make coming to work a joy.

This blogging community has been a miraculous thing in my life. When I told my mom I was making friends on the Internet, I thought she might die of worry. Now I can't imagine my life without it. There are too many inspiring, captivating, and supportive people to name. But let me tell you, if you are wondering if I am talking about you, I am.

Ree and Elise: Thank you for allowing me into your orbits. Your steadfastness and kind hearts make this world and our community a better place.

My editor, Lauren, and the people of Page Street Publishing: Thank you for trusting my vision and pointing me to the way of success.

And with that, I am out.

*Promptly puts on yoga pants, orders a pizza she didn't have to make herself and finally catches up on her Netflix queue.

About the Author

 Megan Keno is a professional recipe developer, food photographer and founder of Country Cleaver, a food blog celebrating the wonders of country living on a small, suburban scale. Her blog and freelance work specialize in multimedia recipe development for commercial and small business, to small and large agriculture enterprises. She works with agricultural cooperatives to raise awareness of the food industry and help people get to know where their food comes from.

Megan's work has been published online, in various print media and on The Pioneer Woman's website Tasty Kitchen, where she was a contributing writer, and Simply Recipes, where her recipes are showcased regularly.

When Megan is not in the kitchen, she works full-time as a project manager for large aviation construction projects and spends time with her husband, Ben, and dog, Huck, in Woodinville, Washington. When they can, they get out of town and head for the rolling wheat fields of eastern Washington. They are also expecting their first child in the fall of 2017.

Index